A Handbook on Open Admissions

The implementation of Open Admissions at CUNY led to the development of a unique program of comprehensive services designed to support the Open Admissions student throughout his or her college career. This book discusses that program, with particular emphasis on Hunter College, supplemented by material on Hostos Community College, the John Jay College of Criminal Justice, and Medgar Evers College.

This book is not merely a compilation of statistical facts and figures, but, rather, an account of the experiences of students, parents, faculty, tutors, peer advisers, administrators, and various other participants in the system. The authors have been at Hunter College since the inception of the Open Admissions policy and have been personally involved with all of the related programs and procedures.

Anne Decker holds a Ph.D. from New York University. She is Assistant Provost for Academic and Admissions Advising at Hunter, and as the college's Coordinator of Programs she is responsible for setting up and coordinating testing, preregistration, advising, and registration for all entering freshmen and advanced-standing students. **Ruth Jody** is Coordinator of Tutorial Services at Hunter College. Formerly a member of Mayor John Lindsay's team on procedures to rehabilitate drug-addicted veterans, she is now completing the requirements for an Ed.D. at Columbia University Teachers College. **Felicia Brings** is Assistant Coordinator of Tutorial Services at Hunter College, where she is currently working toward a master's degree in the Department of Communications.

Westview Special Studies in Higher Education

James R. Davis, *Teaching Strategies for the College Classroom*
Anne E. Decker, Ruth Jody, and Felicia Brings, *A Handbook on Open Admissions*
Ann F. Miller, ed., *A College in Dispersion: Women at Bryn Mawr, 1896-1975*
Allan O. Pfnister, *Planning for Higher Education: Background and Applications*

A Handbook on Open Admissions:

Success, Failure, Potential

Anne Folger Decker
Ruth Jody
Felicia Brings

WESTVIEW PRESS
BOULDER, COLORADO

Published 1976 in the United States of America by
Westview Press, Inc.
1898 Flatiron Court
Boulder, Colorado 80301
Frederick A. Praeger, Publisher and Editorial Director

Library of Congress Cataloging in Publication Data

Decker, Anne.
A handbook on open admissions.

(Westview special studies in higher education)
1. Universities and colleges—United States—Admission. I. Brings, Felicia, joint author.
II. Jody, Ruth, joint author. III. Title.
LB2351.D42   378.1′05′60973   76-7463
ISBN 0-89158-044-1

Printed and bound in the United States of America.

For the students at the Big Apple,
Hunter College,
and Marvin Seiger

CONTENTS

1 Open Admissions: An Overview

> Influences both political and sociological transform
> the University, yet, behind its many changing forms
> looms the timeless ideal of the intellectual insight
> which is supposed to be realized here, yet, which is
> in permanent danger of being lost.
>
> Jasper, *The Ideology of a University*

The concept of Open Admissions is not a new one;
variations of this theme have existed at colleges and
universities throughout the country for quite some time.
Open Admissions means equal access for all to higher
education, even for those individuals whose previous
academic performance and low socioeconomic status
would not ordinarily give them access to college. Con-
troversies still rage, and arguments both for and against
the concept are legion and involve various academic
and social factors. Advocates maintain that higher education promotes social equality and cite the societal responsibilities of the university. Critics argue the matter
on academic grounds and fear for the maintenance of
standards and institutional integrity. For some of those

1

personally involved it has been viewed as an empty promise, a political issue. There is some truth in all these views. Certainly it can be said that the success or failure of any system of Open Admissions cannot be determined without an initial agreement among all concerned about the purpose of the program.

Many midwestern colleges accept all high school graduates, whatever their grade-point averages or SAT (Scholastic Aptitude Test) scores. A weeding-out process begins with the students' first college courses; if they were inadequately trained in high school, it is unlikely that they will suddenly succeed in college. This has been termed "the revolving door" type of Open Admissions policy, and the expectation is that unprepared students will drop out or flunk out before completing the first term or year.

In California, the junior colleges assume the responsibility for training or eliminating underprepared students. The two-year college is viewed as an extension of high school and the natural route for students wishing to enter a four-year college but needing more preparation. If after two years the students have met its standards, they are admitted to the university.

The approach to Open Admissions at the City University of New York (CUNY) has been one of the most interesting experiments in academic history. The CUNY system has attempted fully to reflect the ethnic integration and ever-changing population of New York City. This Open Admissions program (instituted in 1970) has been termed revolutionary, for it is the only one that assumes the responsibility for implementing and financing comprehensive remedial and supportive services designed to help underprepared students succeed in college. The hope has been that the revolving door would remain open, that students would truly have equal opportunity, and that academic standards would be maintained all the while. Achieving this has been a difficult task.

Even before the implementation of Open Admissions, some of the CUNY colleges reflected, by their character, the needs of the communities in which they were located. The advent of Open Admissions to CUNY simply introduced a new student population to several colleges whose nature had been experimental and innovative already.

Education has always been highly valued in New York City, which houses more institutions of higher learning than any other city in the United States. Large numbers of immigrants have settled in New York, poor people who have wanted a better life for their children and seen education as the vehicle for the upward social and economic mobility they sought.

CUNY had its origins in the Free Academy, which was founded in 1847 for male students and became the College of the City of New York (CCNY) in 1866. Tuition was free, and all those who applied were admitted. In 1870 a growing need for public-school teachers transformed the School for Female Monitors into the Normal College and later into Hunter College. The Board of Higher Education was established by the state legislature in 1927 to govern these institutions, which were viewed from the beginning as extensions of the city's free public-school system. Increases in the city's population, along with the changing economic structures following World War I, led to the establishment of academic admissions standards in 1924. Admission became contingent upon a high school average of seventy-two. This was raised to seventy-eight in 1936, eighty-two in 1962, and finally to eighty-five in 1969.

The great social and political pressures of the 1960s led to major restructuring of admissions policy (as well as curriculum, attendance, and numerous other traditional requirements). In 1968 New York City's Master Plan for the City University outlined proposals for the inauguration of Open Admissions in the fall of 1975 as an affirmation of the city's commitment to improving educational opportunities for its poor and minority populations. The original plan called for the following facilities:

1. Senior colleges—four-year colleges including SEEK (Search for Education, Elevation, and Knowledge) program facilities to offer assistance to the hard-core educationally and financially underprepared.

2. Community colleges—two-year schools offering associate degrees and the possibility of transfer to four-year colleges as well as the facilities for a College Discovery Program offering services similar to those of SEEK.

3. Educational skills centers—designed to provide intensive training in academic skills as well as career-oriented technical education for students who have been described as having "potential for the community college career programs and who might have been overlooked in their initial assignment to a City University Institution."

The heated political climate of the '60s necessitated accelerating the implementation of Open Admissions. In the spring of 1969 the Black and Puerto Rican student community took over the South Campus of City College, while a general student strike, accompanied by some violent demonstrations, went into effect. Another significant factor was an upcoming mayoral election, followed in 1970 by a gubernatorial race. At this time city and state budgets were considerably healthier than they are currently, and the timely combination of these factors served as the impetus for the implementation of Open Admissions at CUNY five years before the Master Plan's original schedule. A 1969 amendment to the plan stated:

> The Board of Higher Education proposes an amendment to the 1969 First Revision of the 1968 Master Plan that would expand senior colleges and community colleges enrollments beyond the present goals for the years 1970 through 1975. The Board proposes to expand enrollment goals so that the university may admit a freshman class of 35,000 students in the Fall, 1970 and in each of the subsequent years through 1975 in order to meet the changing needs of the high school graduates of New York City.

The speed with which such an extensive restructuring was to be accomplished necessarily changed some of the originally outlined proposals, and many of the problems of the Open Admissions program can be attributed to this accelerated pace of implementation.

The introduction of an Open Admissions program into the CUNY system engendered an enormous amount of discussion and disagreement about the purpose, validity, and method of the program. Parents, students, faculty, and administrators all had different expectations and opinions. Open Admissions was variously viewed as a "college fixation," an end to academic standards, a temporary solution, and an economic necessity. The program brought together people of different backgrounds and involved them in the process of putting the concept into practice.

The first few months of Open Admissions at Hunter College will be remembered as a time of intellectual and physical chaos. The former was of longer duration, but the latter was of greater impact initially. Inadequate closet and locker space necessitated students and faculty carrying their belongings with them throughout the day. The shortage of classrooms brought classes into the hallways, where students had to sit on the floor for lack of chairs. The most coveted spaces were telephone booths, where a student could study in relative peace and privacy. Rooms changed functions from day to day, with student lounges converted into conference rooms and then into day-care centers in which children used the original lounge furniture as jungle gyms.

As if this were not bad enough, the building itself was being renovated, and besides the usual big city noises, the sounds of construction were a constant part of the school day. Drilling, hammering, and clouds of dust were regular additions to the classroom experience, and during a class a workman's face might suddenly appear where previously there had been a wall. The cafeteria ran out of food, the bookstore ran out of books, and department chairmen worried about where to put students. The decision to accommodate the new students was uppermost in everyone's mind, but the means of doing it were elusive.

It was not only the physical environment that had to be altered, but the academic structure as well. Throughout the first semester established rules had to be examined and revised. This process of revision and reconstitution was complicated by a number of factors. There was no central agency to handle problems. The only place to which a student could go for help was the Dean of Students' Office, whose twelve counselors had neither the time nor the training to cope with all of the students' problems. Previously enrolled students suffered as their problems were overlooked in the process of dealing with the Open Admissions students, and other groups were slighted as well. There was always some group marching outside in protest. When the Black Student Union was granted its demand that more Black and Puerto Rican subjects be accepted in fulfillment of requirements, the Jewish Defense League began clamoring for equal conditions by demanding that Hebrew literature be part of the basic required courses. No fixed doctrine could be developed without the input of all participating members of the college community, and there always had to be room for contingencies.

While the faculty and administration grappled with setting up new rules, revising old ones, and redefining their own roles, the students themselves brought with them visions of what the university should be. Many students came to CUNY believing that college was very different from high school. For many the high school experience had been negative; these students hoped to turn their backs on that part of their lives and start afresh. Others expected college to be simply an extension of high school and very similar in nature. Many students, although they did not know what to expect, thought that a college education ensured a bright and profitable future.

Among the first lessons learned by the Open Admissions student was that everything in college is based on adequate high school preparation and dependent upon basic skills. Many Open Admissions students found that they could not do the course work, that they had the same learning problems in college as in high school. Many students complained that college was just like high school, with requirements to meet and basic skills to master. However, unlike the high school situation, students were not monitored and were responsible for getting their own work done. No one checked to see if assignments were being completed; no tests were given until midterm. In high school every student was eventually graduated, albeit under duress, while in college the student was free to leave, to drop out. It seemed to the students that "nobody cared," and many of them were depressed when their old negative attitudes did not produce the expected professional reaction. Some students responded to these problems by quitting. For those that remained the bright future dimmed, enthusiasm waned, and feelings of inadequacy returned.

Among the most difficult problems of Open Admissions was the students' inability to gauge their own progress; they were often surprised by failing grades. The faculty, too, did not realize that the students were unprepared to evaluate their own work or to seek help when they had problems. Students thought they were doing well, and when questioned they answered, "Everything is fine." It took the faculty a while to recognize that "everything is fine" meant nothing. Teachers had to learn to keep on asking students about their progress and insisting that they get help when needed.

The major problem was an old one carried over from high school, one that the counselors in the Dean of Students' Office were ill equipped to handle: lack of basic skills. It was a matter of students wanting to learn but not having the tools to do so. Both college and student knew in advance that the students were unprepared for college, but neither had realized how large the gap was between the level of skills mastered and the level of skills required. Originally, Hunter had chosen not to identify the Open Admissions students, on the assumption that to do so would be detrimental to their self-esteem. But it became clear that the real detriment was lack of skills, and this would have to be rectified before anything else could be accomplished. A central office, the Office of Academic Advising, was finally established to deal with Open Admissions students.

The Office of Academic Advising provided a number of services and had a variety of functions: it was a place where the Open Admissions students, as well as all of the other students, could ask questions about procedures, a place where official information could be disseminated. The office became a clearinghouse for policies, rules, and regulations. It also provided information on the availability of remedial classes and made sure that students were placed in the appropriate level class. Over time department chairmen worked with the office to distribute information about the total academic program at the college.

The office originally used faculty on release from other duties, but this proved ineffectual since faculty could not give enough time and since such work required intensive training. Eventually several full-time people of varied backgrounds and training were hired to respond to the students' varied needs. The students themselves were helpful in defining and structuring the office, since their questions helped identify problem areas.

It was soon realized that for the student no step is insignificant and that the earlier things are explained, the better prepared the student will be for the next step. It was decided that a student's contact with the advising office should start not at registration, but immediately upon acceptance. Thus, the process began with the day-long placement tests prior to registration. Proctors, who were upperclassmen, answered questions and explained the purpose of the tests, which were aids in placing the students in the proper levels of courses. Academic advisers from the office talked to students about registration procedures. Booklets, entitled "What Every Freshman Should Know," were distributed, and students were encouraged to read the *Bulletin* to help them choose courses. The advisers also recommended that students discuss their individual problems with the appropriate faculty members prior to registration. The entire process of familiarizing students with academic rules and regulations was a developmental one, as we learned, step by step and semester by semester; the task was larger than any of us had anticipated, even after we began to deal with it.

After the semester began, the Office of Academic Advising was always open to students with problems, but we found that even this was insufficient and that we actually needed an entire course in which to disseminate information and help students foresee and forestall common problems. The Freshman Seminar was designed in the fall of 1972 to fulfill these purposes.

The concept of Open Admissions is the result of economic reality, democratic political philosophy, and educational theory. It is not an organic outgrowth of the university system, but rather an attempt to solve a broad range of social, economic, and political problems through education. Traditionally, at the university level the function of education is to transmit complex and specialized information, as well as to discover new knowledge. The Open Admissions program at CUNY broadened immeasurably, though perhaps unwittingly, the demands made upon the university by asking that it fulfill more specific vocational training needs. City University became a funnel into which people of all classes, races, religions, nationalities, and experiences were poured and out of which "college students" emerged. This truly democratic attempt to equalize opportunity through education did not, in its planning stage, take into account the full extent of the task.

College-oriented students—that is, students whose prior training has been predicated on a future college education—reach the university prepared to make a natural progression in education from high school. Basic skills have been mastered, a broad range of academic and nonacademic subjects have been encountered, and university society has been experienced vicariously through siblings, parents, and friends. This preparation for college takes place in school, from nursery through high school, and outside school, at home, on trips, with friends, and in extracurricular activities. Thus, a variety of conditions coincide to produce a college student; economic and intellectual background, cultural traditions, individual experience, and academic preparation all contribute.

The Open Admissions program demanded that CUNY transform non-college-oriented students into successful college students in a matter of months. This was an ambitious undertaking. Open Admissions students walked through the doors of Hunter College with different needs, expectations, and goals. Three types of problems confronted them—personal, financial, and academic. While the three types are related and each is crucial to the potential success of the student, the university could hope to solve only the academic problems. These academic problems, however, were perhaps the least important factor in the creation, implementation, and final restructuring of the Open Admissions program at City University.

Long-term economic and social factors created the conditions that required a program designed to equalize opportunity. Political and economic conditions in the 1960s both demanded and allowed for the development of an Open Admissions policy. Short-term political considerations led to the accelerated implementation of the program five years earlier than was originally planned. Finally, broad political, social, and economic forces modified the Open Admissions policy in 1976. In short, Open Admissions was an academic solution to essentially nonacademic problems.

Americans have always had faith in the efficacy of education as a solution for problems. Education is the American placebo prescribed for all social and individual ills. Particularly in New York City, where the American melting pot is more of a reality than anywhere else, equal access to education, as well as to other social services, is a tradition of long standing. If the university is to have the function of integrator and equalizer, the concept of education must be broadened beyond the academic. Education is but the formal aspect of the larger social process of enculturation, that process which ensures that individual members of a society learn those values, attitudes, and patterns of behavior which constitute a viable culture. This process in no way ignores or negates the ethnic, racial, religious, or economic plurality that characterizes this nation. It only ensures a certain commonality that prevents irreparable rifts. In order to be effective, programs like Open Admissions at CUNY require an enormous amount of thinking, planning, and money. Without an initial recognition of the complexity of the problems, a secure commitment to the goals, and access to the necessary funds, such programs have little chance of success. More important, commitments of time and resources are largely inadequate unless the burden of providing equal opportunity is also spread among all of society's institutions.

2 Expectations

Inherent in a personalized approach to the subject of Open Admissions, which this book endeavors to present, is an examination of the expectations of those individuals most closely affected by it. During the course of preparing this handbook, the authors conducted numerous personal interviews with students and with faculty members. No attempt was made to structure a scientific basis for the survey; what we wanted was an informal compilation of the participants' hopes, fears, and expectations about their involvement in the CUNY experiment. Because Hunter does not label Open Admissions students as such, our criterion for isolating these students was their enrollment in remedial courses.

Interviews with students were conducted with an eye toward perceiving the variety of new expectations they were experiencing as a result of the unplanned-for opportunity to attend college: How did they view college? What were some of the differences among their interpretations of a college education?

Underprepared students who qualify for categorization as Open Admissions students are not limited to any ethnic or racial boundaries. Included among those interviewed were black, Hispanic, West Indian, Asian, and Caucasian students, students of Jewish, Italian, and Irish descent, and students of both sexes. The same twenty-four questions were asked of them all, and what seemed to emerge was a pattern of surprisingly similar, sometimes unrealistic expectations of the college experience.

Question 1: Did any family members or friends attend college before you?

The majority of students answered no to this question. All but one of those with affirmative responses indicated that the people they knew who had attended college were distantly related; the exception was one girl, whose sibling was in attendance at the same time. Not a single one of the students interviewed knew of a member of his or her immediate family or intimate social circle who had attended college in the past.

Question 2: How did they get to go?

Due to the negative responses to question 1, this was considered not applicable.

Question 3: What did you think college was going to be like?

This question brought forth some of the most startlingly similar responses as well as the most patently unrealistic. All of the students interviewed were residents of New York City, and most had been for some time. All of them knew before entering Hunter that the school was located in the center of Manhattan, an area familiar even to nonresidents as a bustling, overcrowded, dirty, noisy, racially mixed urban metropolis. Yet to our amazement, all of the students expressed the expectation that college attendance would somehow mirror the Hollywood image whose *locus classicus* is the Doris Day movie of the 1950s. Students expected a large, quiet, pastoral campus, with mostly white, WASP, well-tailored young people strolling among the trees exchanging a wealth of intellectual ideas while attending a continuous round of football games and proms, replete with cheerleaders, pom-poms, fraternity houses, and homecoming dances in the gym. The only cliché that seemed to have been overlooked was the raccoon coat. One student replied that she entered college because she had nothing better to do and expected to find her future husband there. Generally, the students expected to encounter a great deal of difficult work, but work relating only to subjects that would help them to cope with the world and, specifically, with their intended careers.

Question 4: What was it really like?

It came as no surprise that Hunter did not meet with the expectations described in question 3. Only one student, who had earlier expressed the expectation of encountering hard work and intellectual exchanges, found what she was looking for. Many students were disappointed to find that much of the college environment was simply an extension of what they had experienced in high school; they were incredulous that attendance was taken in many classes and that they were being assigned homework as well as being tested to determine their mastery of the course material. Others expressed disappointment in the intellectual capabilities of their instructors. Many students admitted that, although they had made some new friends, the environment was not as conducive to socializing as they had thought it would be. They were not prepared for the reality of required courses, having been led to believe that one of the best things about going to college would be the freedom to take only those courses they were interested in. Except for the one girl previously referred to, all of the students said that the course work was not as difficult as they had feared and that their work loads were only slightly greater than those they had had in high school. The bureaucratic manner in which the school functions also came as somewhat of a surprise to some students, particularly those who expected that being a college student would bring them greater respect and ease of operation.

Question 5: Are you accomplishing anything by going to college?

Unanimously the students answered yes. Some felt that they were accomplishing intellectual growth, others that they were accomplishing a more secure economic future. One student stated that he was breaking away from poverty and gaining a sense of being able to survive the future, whatever he later chose to pursue. Many students answered yes, but were unable to verbalize what the accomplishments were.

Question 6: What are those of your friends who are not in college doing?

Working in department stores, supermarkets, banks, as secretaries, having babies, on welfare, unemployed. Only one student replied that all of his friends were in college.

Question 7: How do they feel about your being in school?

Most of the answers indicated that friends expressed approval and other positive sentiments such as admiration and envy. One student said that his friends approve of college but are holding off going themselves until they see how it will affect his future employability. Only one student replied that her friends felt that it was a waste of time.

Question 8: Do they want you to spend a lot of time with them, go out, etc.?

The majority replied no; a few said sometimes, but only one student indicated that his friends complained about his never wanting to go out with them and choosing to study instead.

Question 9: Do you stay home and study while your friends go out? If so, does it bother you?

Answers to this question were fairly evenly mixed. Most of the students expressed some mild resentment about staying home to study and indicated that they actually sacrificed socializing only when confronted with an upcoming exam or paper. Two girls replied that they felt very strongly about the importance of their education and that staying home to study was not perceived as a sacrifice.

Question 10: What do you want to do when you graduate?

Replies to this question indicated a surprising (to us) openness and general receptivity to future contingencies. Most of the students had not yet made a career choice and admitted that the reason for this was that they kept hearing that nothing was really available. (These interviews were conducted during March, April, and May of 1976, a period of national recession and very high unemployment.) One girl was firm in her resolution to become a nurse. Only one student expressed a desire to continue on to graduate school. Other replies included the desire to travel, get married, make a lot of money, work with people (albeit without knowing in what particular capacity), and enjoy life.

Question 11: Have your career plans changed as a result of your going to college?

Again, answers were fairly evenly divided, with the yes responses slightly in the lead.

Question 12: Why are you taking the courses you are taking?

The answers to this question indicated that almost unanimously students were taking these courses only to fulfill Hunter's Basic Prescription requirement for a core of liberal arts courses. Only one student (the same one who was planning to attend graduate school) replied that she would have taken a wide variety of courses in different disciplines even if they had not been required.

Question 13: Are your courses helping you in any way?

Despite some of the resentment students expressed at having to take required courses that they were not particularly interested in, all of the students interviewed admitted that these courses were in some way helpful, even the much protested remedial sections. Students replied that they were filling in missing background information; that they were beginning to understand the structure of society; that they were discovering totally new things; that they were learning the indirect causes of various effects; that they were learning how to think and improving their vocabulary. One student indicated that, although she was gaining new ideas, some of it was a waste of time and made no sense at all.

Question 14: Has your life-style changed as a result of going to college?

Here again the answers were almost evenly divided, but the no's were in the majority and some of the yesses were qualified by other factors such as just growing older. Among the yes answers, students said that they were interacting with new and often different kinds of people; that their time was being put to better use than just working and going to bars. One student, an immigrant, replied that college gave her the opportunity to break away from staying with only people from her own ethnic group.

Question 15: Have you made new friends?

The answers were unanimously yes, although several students indicated that acquaintances was a more appropriate description, since relationships seldom continued beyond the semester during which they were developed.

Question 16: Aside from the actual course work, have you learned anything new?

The majority of students answered yes, that they had learned to deal with people and with the system. One student replied that he had found stereotypes often to be untrue and that his exposure to gay people made him learn to accept them as human beings. Only a very few students answered with an unqualified no.

Question 17: Do you talk to your parents about school?

Again, there was an almost equal distribution of answers, with no's in the majority. The yesses indicated that family discussions about school were only cursory; their parents would ask questions such as, "Are you doing OK?" or "Have you decided what you're going to do?" The students who answered no invariably said that their parents would not understand.

Question 18: Do they understand?

This question was either not applicable or had already been answered in question 17, except for one student. She indicated that her father, who had not gone beyond the eighth grade, had desperately wanted her to go to college ever since she was a small child; now he sat spellbound for hours drinking up every detail of her college experience.

Question 19: Do you have your own space in which to study at home?

Most of the students replied no. Only a very few had their own rooms.

Question 20: How much study time do you give to each course?

Answers indicated that time spent in studying was contingent upon the difficulty of the course or the proximity of an exam. Only one student said she gave four to five hours per week on a regular basis to each course.

Question 21: Do you have a job?

Over half of the students did hold part-time jobs.

Question 22: If you will be taking an exam, which is more important, your job or studying for the exam?

All of those students who were employed replied that priority would be given to studying for the exam.

Question 23: Has going to college added any significant experiences to your life?

Answers were unanimously yes. Students indicated that they viewed themselves differently, had more confidence ("I don't take any more jive"), grew emotionally, gained new insights and broadened their understanding, and learned about and accepted different customs of different ethnic and cultural types. One student said that she learned to deal with new attitudes as a result of seeing students smoking marijuana openly and making no attempt to hide it.

Question 24: Do you want to make any comments about college or Open Admissions?

Most of the students expressed approval of the concept of Open Admissions, but felt that college could be improved by removing required courses and being less impersonal. Only one of the interviewees believed that Open Admissions was not a good idea. She felt that admitting underprepared students gives them a sense of anxiety about being in college, and that remediation is not helpful at all; if students were truly motivated, she said, they would attend night school to improve their skills before seeking admission to college.

Frequent informal discussions with students outside the context of a structured interview revealed a general dissatisfaction with the liberal arts orientation of the Basic Prescription requirements for graduation. This very likely reflects a lack of understanding of that orientation. The surprise expressed by so many at the necessity to take courses outside of their interest (career interest, usually) areas indicates a considerable lack in high school preparation (particularly nonscholastic preparation such as counseling) for college entrance. That students whose reading levels are often too low for them to comprehend their textbooks protest remedial courses so vehemently also indicates a disturbing inability of students to make some seemingly obvious academic connections.

A number of faculty members were also interviewed in order to determine some of their expectations and attitudes regarding Open Admissions. Instructors were randomly chosen and many departments were represented. We deliberately chose instructors who had been on staff since before the implementation of Open Admissions in order to establish what changes, if any, their attitudes had undergone, but a few more recent additions to the staff were also included in the survey.

Despite a healthy diversity of opinion among the faculty members interviewed, certain similarities in attitude do emerge. Again, this survey was not rigorous; interviews were often conducted over coffee in the cafeteria or in hallways between classes, and only five questions were asked.

Question 1: Did you support Open Admissions? What were your reasons?

The overwhelming majority of faculty members replied that they had initially supported Open Admissions. Many then modified that affirmative attitude by stating that although they did advocate the concept of Open Admissions they did not support the introduction of the program into the system as it then existed. Many faculty members expressed support for a theoretical Open Admissions policy that included adequate money, space, staff, facilities, preparation time, etc., to ensure its success.

The predominant belief was that everyone deserves an opportunity to receive an education. Some expressed the hope that, through Open Admissions, students would develop a greater need and respect for education. Others believed that there was a need to diversify the student body by the introduction of new and different cultures, or a need to move away from high school records as the criterion for admissions policy. One strong supporter of Open Admissions believed that it was one of the most promising social experiments in the country's history and would provide a situation that more closely approached our democratic ideal of equality of opportunity. Open Admissions was perceived as advantageous to the discipline of education, since it would cause pedagogical problems to surface, would stimulate solutions that were therefore buried or unrecognized, and would extend educators' recognition of different kinds of intelligence and of the variety of learning methods that take place outside the confines of academia.

All of those interviewed expressed concern for the maintenance of academic standards. Only one faculty member, however, expressed vehement opposition to Open Admissions on the grounds that the new student population would be patently unable to do college work, a situation that would ultimately lead to a lowering of standards as well as of the quality of the students. Open Admissions was described by this professor as an altogether ill-conceived policy.

Question 2: What did you think Open Admissions would be like? Did it meet with your expectations or not? Have you changed your opinions about it?

In the replies to the first part of question 2, the word "chaos" was used repeatedly to describe the situation that faculty members expected as a result of the implementation of Open Admissions. One associate professor argued that the chaos would be the natural result of a procedure for which no one was prepared and for which there had been inadequate planning. Some thought that the advent of Open Admissions would be catastrophic, basing that opinion on what they had heard from colleagues in other schools. A number of instructors, however, who were confused and disturbed about the program's chances for success, professed to have no preconceived notions about the experiment and admitted that they had no frame of reference from which to base any initial judgment. One interviewee who expected a chaotic situation also felt that it was an extremely promising and personally fascinating experiment. Another believed that, educationally, little could be accomplished apart from bringing some borderline students up to a barely passing level. Many professors laughed at the question and dismissed the entire idea as being a ridiculous one and not worth commenting upon. Only one idealist expected real progress and change that he was able to verbalize in specific terms. He expected that as a result of Open Admissions people who had never understood the value of education would realize that it was advantageous. He expected that incoming students would really be interested in working and in learning and that, therefore, there would be no resistance. He felt, too, that Open Admissions students would prove to be highly motivated because of their realization that getting an education is, after all, better than being on the street. Interestingly, this instructor, more vehemently than most of the others, felt that his expectations had not been fulfilled and that, in fact, the majority of Open Admissions students managed to get through high school merely by sitting in a chair and wanted to get through college the same way. He also interpreted their benign neglect of study as an indication of their hostility, which, because they were too intimidated to express openly, they masked with a show of boredom.

Most of the faculty who expected the system to fail felt that it had. They saw the fulfillment of their expectations in the fact that students were being graduated who were unable to read or write; academic standards had not been maintained at all. One professor complained that a fraud was being perpetrated in allowing students to believe that a B.A. degree would lead to better employment. As a result of this, he felt, unqualified students were enrolling in increasing proportions—and the institution was making things entirely too easy for these students.

Overall, very few of those interviewed admitted to having had their initial opinions changed after five years of seeing the system in operation. Those who originally supported the concept of Open Admissions stated that they continued to do so, provided that there were adequate resources to ensure success. They believed that the lack of funds with which to provide adequate remediation was the cause of the system's apparent failure, and that given more money, more space, more advance planning and preparation, there was no reason that Open Admissions could not become a viable reality.

Question 3: Do you have any suggestions for improving either Open Admissions or the quality of college life in general at Hunter?

One suggestion for improving the system emerged most often, albeit in various forms: that some sort of structured preparatory training—between high school and college—be established. Although some professors believed that it was entirely feasible for the college to offer remedial instruction, the majority thought that it had no place within the college and came up with numerous proposals for some type of interim program that would give highly motivated underprepared students an opportunity to improve their skills and develop a sense of what would be expected of them in college. Most instructors called for much more comprehensive remedial instruction. Others suggested improving campus conditions by creating more physical space; one professor replied that being in a commuter college put great stress on the students and that the overcrowded conditions made the environment even more alienating. Many faculty members suggested that too much pressure was being put on students to get a college degree and that a recognition of alternate skills would be more helpful than allowing students to maintain false impressions of what a college education could do for them.

Question 4: What have been the effects of Open Admissions on your department? On Hunter? Have they generally been good or bad?

Surprisingly, a great many replies indicated mixed feelings on the part of even the most critical professors as to the effect of Open Admissions on the institution and on their departments. Those with initially a total opposition to the system, however, did express a perception of only negative effects. One member of the sociology department pointed out that the introductory sociology course had been transformed into a sort of glorified high school social science course; the only effects that might possibly be interpreted as positive were the opportunity for professors to put in less effort now than they usually did and an increase in the number of teaching positions available. Overall, his position was that Open Admissions led to a restructuring of courses to meet the needs of the new students and that this, in turn, led to a dilution of educational quality and a loss of academic criteria.

Instructors from most departments complained that among the greatest problems engendered by Open Admissions was the coddling of students through relaxed standards and grade inflation. A large number of professors, however, admitted that Hunter and their individual departments had flourished because of the increased number of minority students; these students provided new perspectives that, despite the great problems they brought with them, were generally healthy and good for the institution. One member of the English department observed that Hunter's new problems were more the fault of overcrowding than they were of the new student population. Another instructor believed that Open Admissions imbued Hunter with more beauty as well as more ugliness than any other college in the United States and that the effects of this were generally positive ones. One professor believed that Hunter was not as vibrant as it once had been; that it used to be a finer institution for learning when it had good, motivated students, but that the new system provided excellent training for teachers in difficult situations; it also helped to create new jobs, thereby stimulating the economy.

Many faculty members complained that Open Admissions was responsible for the granting of phoney (worthless) diplomas and for raising students' expectations to a point that was more harmful than helpful. Yet, another sentiment as frequently expressed was that possibly the small improvement Open Admissions made in people's lives was worth the problems it brought. There seemed to be a feeling that Open Admissions at CUNY works theoretically but not practically; that it has wreaked havoc but has also improved the quality of numerous lives.

Question 5: What do you think we should do in the future?

Again and again, the issue of more money was raised in response to this question, along with repetitions of answers to previous ones. Advocated repeatedly were preparatory training situations that would improve basic skills while teaching students what to expect of college, better screening out of unqualified students, more thorough remediation, more individualized counseling, more physical space, no pushing students through school for political reasons, more intelligent presentation of ideas, orientation sessions before classes begin, etc. Almost all of the suggestions were, of course, contingent upon a much healthier economy. Even the harshest critics admitted that money could conceivably provide the opportunity to fill the educational gaps of underprepared students.

3 The CUNY System

Equal educational opportunities became a volatile issue in the student unrest of the 1960s. CUNY responded to the needs of its New York City population by endorsing the establishment of a number of new colleges that would accommodate the increasing numbers of students who wished to enter college and by responding to the particular needs of various student groups.

In 1961 New York State's Education Law was amended to incorporate City College, Hunter College, Brooklyn College, Queens College, Staten Island Community College, Bronx Community College, and Queensborough Community College into a single unit known as City University of New York. CUNY continued to grow during the '60s with the creation of the Graduate Center, John Jay College of Criminal Justice, York College, Richmond College, Medgar Evers College, and four additional community colleges: Borough of Manhattan Community College, Fiorello H. La Guardia Community College, Kingsborough Community College, and Eugenio Maria de Hostos Community College. During this period of social upheaval the university became increasingly aware of its

29

responsibility to the ethnically, culturally, and economically diverse population of the city it served, and it affirmed its desire to change along with the times. As the Wagner Commission reported:

> In a very real sense the mission of the City University has paralleled that of New York City. Both have served as gateways to opportunity for successive waves of newcomers. CUNY's development is tied to New York City's in other ways as well. Through all its stages, CUNY's geographical pattern of development has paralleled that of the city itself. New campuses have followed the shifting demographics of the city.

The implementation of Open Admissions was, then, the logical extension of a system that had, traditionally, provided free, quality higher education to those who could not afford to attend private institutions. Open Admissions sought to provide those in the lower socio-economic groups with access to education, economic success, and general upward mobility.

Originally, plans for the implementation of Open Admissions included study skill centers—somewhat akin to prep schools—as well as the new community colleges. The Harlem community pressured for a program called SEEK, which operated independently of the university system, but which could be attached to each college. SEEK (Search for Education, Elevation, and Knowledge) was established as another alternative to all-out aid for disadvantaged students. It provides courses, tutoring, stipends, and ample counseling services needed by these students, who must withstand considerable pressures at home.

The colleges and programs that came into being along with the new Open Admissions policy reflect, by their character, the reasons for their establishment. Those reasons, as do the schools themselves, differ. CUNY is not a monolithic institution, and the schools described here (both two year and four year) fulfill uniquely the traditional role of the community college: to respond to the needs of its particular community (as the nomenclature suggests).

In spite of the centralization of administrative governance, the CUNY colleges were left to themselves to function as independent units with only general guidelines for the development of programs to help underprepared students. Each college responded to existing needs. Since the deficiencies of most of the student population were the result of academic neglect (among other factors), all of the colleges came up with similar basic ground rules. They each developed some form of tutorial assistance—individual as well as group—and new audiovisual materials. All of the schools eventually concluded that tutoring alone was insufficient; that filling educational gaps was not enough and that an organized effort had to be made to *teach* the missing skills. Most of the colleges established remedial programs and attempted to approach teaching in these programs in as different a manner from that employed in the high schools as was possible. Every college eventually developed remedial programs in basic reading, writing, and arithmetic, and many sought to provide mathematical-reasoning (logic) courses for the sciences.

All of the CUNY schools were faced with the problems of appropriate placement of students. Once entrance requirements and SAT scores were discarded, it became apparent that there had to be some measurement of academic skills, so placement tests were devised and administered by the schools. More comprehensive academic-advising systems were developed to clarify for disgruntled and often quite angry students the reasons for their having to take remedial courses in what they considered to be high school subjects.

All of the CUNY colleges made serious efforts to make Open Admissions succeed and developed innovative programs responsive to community needs. There were, for example, ethnic programs for La Guardia's Chinese population, large federally funded veterans programs at Brooklyn College and City College, and prisoners programs at almost all of the community colleges. Medgar Evers College, John Jay College of Criminal Justice, and Hostos Community College, however, constructed programs that most directly reflected the needs of their populations. Since all three of these schools were developed for a special purpose, their faculties were particularly willing and able to work with the new system; they did not have to alter previously established methods. Faculty, administration, community leaders, and students worked together from their schools' inceptions and geared much of their energy toward self-evaluation, criticism, and the development of a relevant philosophy, although this emphasis sometimes clouded the original definition and purpose of a university.

Medgar Evers College

Medgar Evers College, named after the slain civil rights leader, offers both two- and four-year degree programs. Located in Bedford-Stuyvesant, one of the most neglected, impoverished, and crime-ridden areas in Brooklyn, it is flanked by Williamsburg (populated largely by Hassidic Jews) and by numerous Caribbean and Haitian neighborhoods. The area was ripe for a college and a community center of its own, which is what Medgar Evers has supplied. A university building is currently under construction; meanwhile the school utilizes various buildings, warehouses, churches, temples, etc.

From its inception in September 1971 Medgar Evers has sought to provide students with a comprehensive liberal arts education along with very specific career training. Career choices are defined so that the student can work toward a visible, concrete goal. The admissions policy permits the acceptance of students both from within the community and from outside who have expressed a desire to specialize in any of the school's particular career areas. Advisers encourage students to make an early commitment to career goals so that they can receive vocational training while pursuing the traditional liberal arts education.

Entering students take a placement exam and are assigned to a program specifically designed for their individual needs. English and math, both tailored to students' skill levels, and individual or group tutoring sessions are worked right into their schedules in advance. All scheduling of classes is done by the college (in contrast to Hunter, where students are responsible for scheduling their own programs). Counseling is also written into the program, as are other supportive services, and is mandatory. Students are able, after two years, to receive an associate degree and/or be trained and eligible for a full-time job, but may also elect to continue in school toward the achievement of a four-year degree. During the second two years they have much greater flexibility in choosing suitable courses and hours.

All courses are taught by the regular faculty, so that students study remedial math, for example, with the same instructor who teaches the college-level math courses; remedial specialists are not used.

What most aptly characterizes Medgar Evers College is its concentration on vocational programs that relate to urban needs and particularly to those of its surrounding communities. Nursing, public administration, business education, and teacher education are career areas that the Bedford-Stuyvesant and surrounding communities have designated the most significant and having the greatest opportunity potential, so the college concentrates on vocational education in these fields. The community, then, lets the school know which professions can best serve its needs, and graduates trained for these professions generally have the best chance of finding employment within the community.

The college has a Community Council made up of community leaders and elected officials who participate in important policy decisions and maintain the exceptionally close ties between the school and the needs of central Brooklyn. Medgar Evers works closely with the National Alliance of Businessmen, which donates its members' time and experience to help develop a curriculum that will develop potential skills and employability in inner-city youths. The community has benefited from the replacement of unskilled labor by skilled workers—the change has encouraged expansion and increased the area's financial gains.

The community's influence on the school has permitted the development of a curriculum that allows students to work in their chosen fields while attending classes. In-service programs are available in local schools, businesses, and hospitals, all extensions of the college's emphasis on achieving tangible success. Education at Medgar Evers is not confined to the classroom; as much time, money, and thought goes into counseling, job placement, and community-based experience as goes into academic instruction. The rationale is always clearly evident: education in itself is of little use unless it leads somewhere.

The average age of Medgar Evers' students is twenty-six or twenty-seven. Their life experience and "street wisdom" is recognized, appreciated, and utilized in determining course structures, as is the fact that many of them are working and supporting families. The Business and Secretarial Sciences Division has an internship program that allows some students to work full time for an accounting firm for two months at salaries of $700 per month.

Medgar Evers' Teacher Education Program gives prospective teachers two years of student-teaching experience instead of the traditional one year. Students work in community schools, with special preparation for dealing with the problems of inner-city schools. Nursing students, too, concentrate on the special needs of both the inner-city nurse and the inner-city patient, with course work aimed at promoting a better understanding of black and Hispanic family concepts.

Hostos

Another of the new CUNY schools whose character has been largely influenced by its location, its political nature, and its student/community population is Eugenio Maria de Hostos Community College. Situated in the South Bronx, an area characterized by crime, unemployment, and poverty, Hostos also emphasizes the development of vocational skills necessary for achieving social and economic upward mobility for its students and its community.

Named after the Puerto Rican writer and educator, Hostos tailors many of its programs to suit the needs of its predominantly Spanish-speaking constituency. It attempts to promote its students' ethnic consciousness with comprehensive course offerings in its Department of Puerto Rican Studies as well as its Department of Black Studies.

Upon entering Hostos Community College, one is immediately struck by the easygoing, comfortable, yet purposeful ambience. The students are somewhat older (median age is twenty-seven) than at most universities and are made to feel more at home here because a lack of fluency in English does not, as is often the case elsewhere, automatically categorize them as illiterate. Many of the introductory-level courses are taught in Spanish as well as in English; signs and posters are written in Spanish, and even the telephone operators answer in both languages.

Hostos was established in 1970 for the express purpose of serving the South Bronx community. The faculty are well aware of the institution's meaning and its purpose; they know why they are there and do not generally feel that they were hired in order to perform impossible tasks. Faculty and students share common, well-defined goals, and work exceptionally well together. Both understand the problems of the community and of the educational system that has failed to serve their needs. Administrators at Hostos do not measure success in terms of how long a student's education may take, nor is failure defined by a student's lack of skills at the entrance point. What counts at Hostos is the knowledge, and the ability to apply it practically, that the student has acquired by the time he or she is ready to leave.

Instruction is based on a systems approach. The assumption from the beginning is that the student, being unprepared, is not even aware of the most basic requirements. Instructors are responsible for letting students know at the start what is expected of them, why subjects are taught, and for what practical purpose. Every course is divided into "milestones," each of which has a "performance objective." Students must pass exams upon completion of each milestone before continuing on to the next one. Credit for the course is given upon successful completion by the student, who is "in progress" until this is achieved. The system, designed by Hostos's President Candido de Leon, rewards success while it reduces feelings of failure or anxiety among students who are unable to progress at a rapid pace. Instructors approach their subject matter from a level that most of the students are familiar with; they proceed upward from there, and work individually with students after class hours. Hostos has an Instructional Resources Division that consists of a traditional college library as well as self-paced audiovisual material, much of which is faculty generated.

The systems approach actually combines into one integral unit such services as counseling, advising, career planning, tutoring, and teaching. It maintains fluid connections between education and pragmatic applications—between what the student learns and the reality of his peculiar situation and his career goal. Because the Hostos student is older and more career oriented, he understands material better as what he learns is meaningful to him. Students are told what is expected of them academically and how much study time probably goes into the accomplishment of that. They are taught how the various job functions they will have to perform fit together, and that many of these functions will not be what the students expect. When nursing students raise questions such as "Why must I take chemistry?" they are not made to feel ignorant by an instructor's unwitting look of incredulity or condescension. Faculty are prepared for such questions; indeed, the answers are often built into the curriculum in advance.

All incoming students take placement tests in English and math, and, before they begin their course work, students requiring remediation receive intensive tutoring by regular faculty as well as upper-level students. The bilingual approach is particularly relevant to the school's wide variety of students, who come from varied (although generally Hispanic) backgrounds. Some Hostos students are graduates of New York City high schools, coming from

Spanish-speaking homes, and have absorbed the cultural characteristics implicit in the American urban high school experience at its worst along with the quite different cultural regulations imposed by the family. Others are those who have recently emigrated from small villages, whose parents are illiterate, and who have no fluency in English or Spanish. Some students are graduates of Latin American high schools and simply do not speak English, while others have recently arrived in the United States, gone immediately to work, and speak only "job" English. Hostos has taken this diversity into consideration in structuring its curriculum, and the mix seems to work. Intensive instruction is available in both English and Spanish. Inability to speak English does not prevent students from being trained for careers, particularly in the health fields. Like central Brooklyn, the South Bronx needs graduates to work in the community, and a concerted effort is made by everyone involved to expedite this kind of relevant learning.

Hostos's extracurricular supportive services include massive tutoring utilizing advanced students, alumni, and volunteers from other CUNY colleges. Technology is relied upon heavily in Hostos's math, reading, and writing labs. The remedial program in the physical sciences is extensive, since many students train for the health professions; such courses as physics for x-ray technicians and chemistry for nurses are offered, and instructors are usually available to students beyond the required regular office hours.

Hostos's Division of Health Services is particularly closely associated with community institutions and is a major participant in the drive to alleviate some of the South Bronx's health-care problems. Students can follow career programs in pediatric care, medical laboratory technology, medical secretarial skills, nursing, dental hygiene, and x-ray technology. Several community-based health-care institutions offer their facilities to enable students to obtain clinical experience. A free clinic, operated by Hostos's Dental Hygiene Program, provides patients with such services as instruction on dental care, cleaning, and fluoride application.

The Division of Continuing and Community Education at Hostos has recently developed a Minority Small Business Program. This program provides an opportunity for local businessmen who operate community stores and service organizations to learn to deal with such basics as alternate financing, suppliers, distributors, sales, record keeping, and advertising. Upon completion of the course of study students receive a certificate rather than an associate's degree. Students are often referred to the program by the Puerto Rican Forum or the Small Business Administration.

All of the CUNY community colleges offer courses for the elderly, but Hostos is the only school to offer its courses in Spanish. The Institute of Study for Older Adults provides requested instruction for senior citizens in their homes as well as in senior citizen centers. There are also a number of students in attendance at Hostos who are inmates of the Greenhaven Correctional Facility (a maximum security state prison) and who participate in the school's Study-Release Program.

Perhaps even more than Medgar Evers College, Hostos is characterized by a sense of unity in its objectives and its philosophical approach to education. The major emphasis is always on developing resources that will ultimately provide the South Bronx and, indeed, New York City, some much-needed community services.

The John Jay College of Criminal Justice

The John Jay College of Criminal Justice, located in midtown Manhattan, is another of the new CUNY colleges whose character has been shaped by its role in the community and by its student constituency. John Jay was established in 1965, not because of the imminent implementation of Open Admissions, but, rather, in response to a growing need for widening communications between law enforcement agencies and the public. Although numerous civilian students are in attendance at John Jay, its student body is comprised largely of police officers, firemen, and other municipal, state, and federal law enforcement agents, as well as prisoners, ex-offenders, and prison guards. Fully accredited as one of CUNY's senior colleges, the school offers both liberal arts and specialized education in criminology. There are B.S. and B.A. programs in police science, criminal justice, forensic science, fire science and administration, and social science, and graduate programs leading to master's degrees in public administration, social relations, criminal justice, psychology, and forensic science. John Jay also offers an associate degree program in government and administration, in cooperation with the Port of New York Authority.

Originally called the College of Police Science, the school's name was changed in 1966 in honor of the first chief justice of the Supreme Court. The Open Admissions policy of the City University has had a drastic effect on John Jay, whose student body has increased from 2,000 to 10,500 since 1969. Part of John Jay's unique character is attributable to the fact that so many of its students have already chosen careers and are, in fact, full-time working professionals; the educational emphasis there is on life enrichment rather than vocational training.

As police officers and fire fighters usually work erratic shifts, John Jay schedules its courses at odd hours in order to accommodate their special needs. Identical programs are offered morning and evening (both sections are taught by the same instructor), and students may attend either session, alternating as their duty shifts change. This schedule has benefited all of the students, especially women whose family responsibilities might otherwise interfere with their ability to attend classes regularly.

The need of John Jay students to develop their reading and writing skills has brought into existence the school's Department of Communication Skills (CSD). Entering students submit a writing sample and take a reading test, the outcome of which determines their placement into one of the first two levels of the department's course offerings. The first-level course emphasizes intensive work in reading comprehension, vocabulary, and organization. The second level is designed for students whose reading comprehension is adequate but who need to develop proper study skills: using the library, taking notes, outlining, etc. Each course offers one credit. Only the first level (reading comprehension) is mandatory, although students whose test scores place them at the second level are strongly encouraged to enroll. A third level, designed to help students structure their reading skills around thematic applications, has recently been added to the program. This course, too, offers one credit; students are graded on a pass-fail basis. The department also operates a communication skills laboratory for students unable to participate in the regular courses. Lab instructors are available to deal with specific reading difficulties, while at the same time they can give students individualized counseling sessions. Students may come to the lab for help as often as they deem it necessary.

Other resources available to John Jay students include a comprehensive tutoring service, staffed by graduate students and CSD faculty members, and a Mathematics Resources Center. The center offers review workshops for students ill prepared for advanced courses; it utilizes filmstrips, audio tapes, written materials, calculators, and computers, as well as tutors, to assist students in learning and understanding mathematical concepts.

John Jay also offers an innovative baccalaureate degree program under the auspices of its newly created Thematic Studies Program (TSP), which allows for an alternate means of fulfilling traditional curriculum requirements. Students enrolled in TSP take only one thirty-credit course during the academic year. That one course, however, combines subject matter from a variety of disciplines and makes particular use of New York City as an educational resource. Each of the courses offered is taught by a team of six to eight professors and counselors, supplemented by audiovisual technology as well as prestigious guest lecturers from New York's social and political arenas. During 1974-75 the following three TSP courses were taught:

The Exceptional Person: A Study of Genius, Creativity, Deviance, and Differentness.

The Urban Experience: What Man Has Done to the City and What the City Has Done for Man.

America: Ideals and Realities.

In keeping with its commitment to public service in New York City, John Jay has several programs geared to promote academic excellence among professionals in the criminal justice fields. In keeping with this it is headquarters for the Secretariat for the Academy of Criminal Justice Sciences, the American Association for Professional Law Enforcement, the International Criminal Justice Speakers Consortium, and the Family Crisis Intervention Program. The school has recently introduced a community-based, adult education project known as the Satellite Program. Designed for civil service employees, the program affords working adults an opportunity to achieve college diplomas at locations convenient to their homes or places of employment. Classes are held at several police precinct stations and fire stations throughout New York City, and, as in the main building, classes are scheduled to accommodate rotating shifts. Other unique features of the community-oriented education offered at John Jay are instruction in self-protection for senior citizens, Spanish-language instruction for New York City hospital personnel, and a program that trains "unemployables" to work as security guards.

4 Open Admissions at Hunter

Thomas Hunter, from whom Hunter College takes its name, arrived in this country from Ireland in 1850 and became known as a gifted teacher, an able administrator, and an honest and outspoken man. When the Female Normal and High School opened its doors on February 14, 1870, Hunter was its first president, and the school was the first institution for the education of teachers in New York City and among the earliest institutions of higher learning for women in the United States. The staff consisted of Hunter, a woman superintendent, and four professors. Classes were held on the second floor of a rented loft building at Fourth Street and Broadway.

A permanent site was soon chosen at Sixty-eighth Street and Park Avenue, although many objected to a school for girls on the outskirts of the city, and in 1873 the students moved into their new Gothic-style home. The first course was a three-year program, later extended to four. By 1908 Normal College offered a four-year academic course with a fully accredited Bachelor of Arts degree.

Under the presidency of George Samler Davis, who succeeded Thomas Hunter, the college became Hunter College in 1914, instituted a summer session two years later, and began evening and extension sessions the following year. In 1920, during its Golden Jubilee, the college received its charter from Phi Beta Kappa. In 1926, Hunter along with other city colleges was placed under the jurisdiction of the Board of Higher Education. During the term of James M. Kieran, president from 1929 to 1933, the Bronx buildings were constructed, where freshman and sophomore courses were offered.

Eugene A. Colligan became the next president and extensively revised the curriculum and administration. During 1939 the present democratic organization of the faculty and of all departments was introduced. Another change grew out of an event no one could foresee: in 1936, on the morning of the college's sixty-sixth birthday, the old Gothic structure burned, and classes had to be continued in temporary quarters. October 1940 simultaneously celebrated the inauguration of Hunter's fifth president, George N. Shuster, and the dedication of its new sixteen-story building on the Sixty-eighth Street site.

The college kept pace with the changing times. During World War II the thirty-acre Bronx campus was turned over to the Navy as a training center for the WAVES. The U.S.S. Hunter became a familiar name throughout the country, but the college was destined for world renown. In March 1946, the United Nations Security Council convened for the first time in the United States; the meeting was held on the Hunter uptown campus, and the name of the college was carried around the world. Security Council sessions were held there through August, until the United Nations moved to larger quarters to Lake Success. Meanwhile, plans were made for the reopening of Hunter in the Bronx.

Another major change was on the way. The citizens of the Bronx had urged that a full four-year division of the college, for both men and women students, be established in the borough, and a study made by a faculty committee in 1950 revealed a strong demand on the part of high school students for such a center. Thus, in the fall of 1951, the Bronx Division of Hunter College became a four-year, coeducational institution. A School of General Studies offering evening courses opened in February 1961.

The curriculum of both divisions of the college expanded to include the varied courses leading to the A.B., B.S., and B.F.A. degrees, as well as graduate courses leading to the M.A. and M.S. degrees. In 1964 the day session of the Park Avenue Division became coeducational. Four years later the Bronx campus became a separate unit of the City University of New York, which had been organized in April 1961 to administer all of the public higher-education institutions in the city, and was renamed Herbert H. Lehman College. Still remaining as part of the Hunter family are the elementary school and the high school, both serving as demonstration schools and research facilities for the teacher education program.

As a logical extension of the Open Admission's policy, CUNY offered admission to senior citizens aged sixty-five and older on a space available basis in the spring of 1973. Hunter also offers noncredit adult education courses of general interest to the community through its Center for Lifelong Learning.

Hunter's reaction to the new set of problems introduced by the adoption of the Open Admissions policy by the Board of Higher Education was based on the recommendations of its Faculty Committee on Open Admissions, appointed to propose ways in which to prepare for the new program. The committee developed what seemed to them a reasonable approach to dealing with poorly prepared students while preserving the essence of Hunter's academic program. Their initial attitudes were tempered by their awareness that the academic level of the incoming students was unknown and that the traditional offering of single entry points for new freshmen was unrealistic. However, multiple entry points, geared to the varying degrees of preparation of individual students, required personalized academic advising for all incoming students. Otherwise, it would be difficult to make the new students aware of all the available options open to them and to ensure proper placement.

In line with this approach, the committee made their recommendations. They agreed that students should be encouraged to take courses building on their strengths and interests so that their initial college experience would be one of success. The college should support this effort by modifying the curriculum where possible to provide opportunities for demonstrating the relationship between the academic world and the world outside the college. The committee believed that many of the incoming students had experienced many facets of life but did not know how to relate these experiences to conceptual principles and therefore draw conclusions from their experiences that could be generalized to other areas. The committee therefore recommended that attempts be made to invert the normal classroom procedure whereby principles are presented and experiential data then accumulated to support them. Another recommendation was that grading policies allow students more time than usual to demonstrate competence, as well as an opportunity to explore heretofore unknown subjects without penalty. The means for doing this would be the institution of a "Y" grade, permitting students to take a year to complete course work that normally would have been done in one semester. The "Y" grade would indicate that the student was indeed trying, but had not been able to achieve the exit criteria at the same rate as some of the other members of the class and was being given an additional amount of time to do so. Finally, the committee concluded that remediation should be a "voluntary commitment on the part of the student." Students should be given the option of choosing a remedial program after considering both the pitfalls if it was avoided and the probable rewards from its successful completion. The college should provide extensive support services, especially in the form of tutoring and advising, so that underprepared students would not be consigned to the "second-class citizenship" of remediation. The intention was that Open Admissions students would not be separated from the regularly admitted students, but rather that the academic departments themselves would assume the responsibility of providing necessary backup services as integral parts of their first-level course offerings. We could not, of course, have known it at that time, but this well-intentioned position proved to be unrealistic and impractical and was to undergo several changes in the ensuing years.

Before Open Admissions all applicants to Hunter had to have high school diplomas with a prescribed distribution of English, science, mathematics, language, and history courses, together with at least an eighty-five grade-point average in these courses or satisfactory SAT scores. With the advent of Open Admissions the criteria for entrance were completely overhauled. The courses comprising the students' high school program were no longer important, as long as the students had a diploma or a GED (General Equivalency Diploma) from New York State.

Students were allocated to Hunter by the CUNY Office of Admissions Services, a central admissions office established to service the entire university. Any student with no prior college work submitted a single application to the office, indicating his or her first six choices of colleges. The computer branch of the office, the University Application Processing Center (UAPC), took these applications and made the actual allocations to the various community and senior colleges, attempting to give as many students as possible their first choice. The two benchmarks used to determine school assignment were the student's grade-point average and his or her percentile ranking in class. The UAPC matched first choices with the number of seats each college had available, and the computer established the grade-point-average cut points that provided the best fit. A second run was then made to pick up unallocated students by their class ranking, thus allowing some students with low averages but high class standings to get their first choice of college. All other unallocated students were then assigned according to their choices and the seats left in the colleges.

For the six years of Open Admissions Hunter's grade-point-average cut point has ranged between about eighty-two and eighty-five, and the class-ranking cut point has been between the sixty-eighth and seventy-fifth percentiles. In addition, in recent years a group of below-seventy-average students has been arbitrarily allotted to Hunter and some of the nine other senior colleges in order to equalize the mix of students in the colleges that have high cut points. The cut points are determined by supply and demand, and some of the senior colleges, like Hunter, Queens, and Brooklyn, have had many more applicants than they can accommodate. Certain career programs in some of the community colleges, for example nursing and hotel and restaurant management, have been in high demand; and the health profession baccalaureate programs have been flooded with applicants. The UAPC, therefore, has had to set limitations for determining acceptance into these programs. At the same time, all of the colleges have expanded their capacities, beginning in 1970, in order to try to accommodate the expanded college population. Hunter, for example, almost doubled its undergraduate student body in four years, adding crowding and lack of space to the problems to be dealt with under this new policy.

The criteria for September 1976 entrants have been modified so that a minimum grade-point average of eighty and class ranking in the upper third are necessary for admission to a senior college, while a seventy grade-point average and the twenty-fifth percentile permit entry into a community college. Students who do not meet these standards will be given the opportunity of attending transitional centers in which they will be given help to work toward matriculation.

How then did Hunter react to some of the problems brought about by these changes? Philosophically, it has supported the basic premise that students' pasts should not be held against them, that the college should do everything possible to help the underprepared students bring themselves to the point where they can successfully complete a college curriculum. Educationally, it has insisted that standards must be maintained, that course content cannot be diluted, and that social promotion benefits no one—neither the students falsely promoted nor those who worked hard for their degrees. Pragmatically, it has tried many approaches, discarded some, modified others, kept a few, and continually searched for better ways to keep Open Admissions from being an empty promise.

The following chapters describe some of these efforts, in the hope that they will save wear and tear on future administrators who may be faced with similar situations.

5   Testing

Like Topsy, the testing program at Hunter "just grew." At first there was nothing. The Board of Higher Education administered a battery of tests called the Open Admissions Tests during the spring of 1970 and again in the spring of 1971 to all New York City high school students. One interesting feature of these tests was an indication by the students themselves as to whether or not they believed they needed help in reading, writing, or mathematics. These data could have been valuable, but were not used at Hunter in any formal way since we had decided against remedial courses. Hunter did no testing on its own.

One of the reasons the college moved slowly toward testing was embedded in the college's history. Before 1970 the burden of proof for entrance eligibility had been on the student: applicants were responsible for proving to the college by their past performance that they were probably capable of college-level work and therefore acceptable for admission.

After Open Admissions the burden of proof shifted from the applicants to the college. Rather than anticipating freshmen with a fairly homogeneous preparation, Hunter was confronted with a heterogeneity of unknown quantities and qualities. Because the college could not take into account the entering students' past performance or preparation in specific areas, it had to guess about where to place them in first-semester courses or else use the only piece of data available, namely their high-school grade-point averages. Only at the end of the first semester could a standard judgment—grades—be made, and by then many mistakes might already have been made.

The English department decided to act on its own to modify this uncertainty. First, it developed a preparatory course for students who needed additional writing instruction, and it tested all the entering students once school began. This testing and sorting into proper levels consumed almost three weeks of the term, shortening the time available for class work. It also showed that testing in advance of registration was the only way to avoid wasting valuable instructional time. Likewise, later feedback from the other academic departments indicated that some better way had to be devised for advising students not to register in classes for which they were unprepared.

Plans were therefore made to conduct at least a modicum of testing in the spring of 1971 for the class entering in September. Tests were given in English structure and mechanics, reading comprehension, and second-language problems, along with an essay to be scored by the English faculty. In addition, students were given the option of taking other tests as placement aids: reading and oral tests for students who had taken French or Spanish in high school and wished to continue the language in college; a calculus readiness test; and a test covering the material often presented in twelfth-grade mathematics, offering students a chance to earn three college credits prior to entrance (similar to Advanced Placement credits offered in conjunction with special courses in many high schools). The results of these tests were ready for June registration.

A testing program like this necessitated the hiring of proctors. Upperclassmen who had been active in student activities were recruited and given a two-hour briefing before the testing weekend. The testing was done on a weekend because that was the only time classrooms were free and also the only time that the entering students would not have to cut their own high school classes. The freshmen gathered in the auditorium in the morning for information about the tests and about Hunter's program and requirements; they were then sent to the testing classrooms for the rest of the day. They had been told to bring their lunch; the college supplied cold drinks, and the proctors ate lunch with the new students to try to make them feel somewhat at home.

There were, of course, problems. The general and special tests were given only once in the spring. All entrants who missed the tests, or who were accepted after the testing weekend, had to be placed without the benefit of the tests. Except for the basic writing courses, the test results were no more than advisory. When students disputed the results or indicated a belief that they could handle a given course, their belief in their own capability by and large outweighed test indications.

The situation changed dramatically with the institution of remedial courses for the fall 1972 entering class (see chapter 7). Testing then became crucial for placement, and the battery was expanded to include tests for mathematics skills as well as for reading and writing. We tried an additional test for students with second-language problems, but the complications of giving it were not worth the results.

Thus, during the second year of testing (the third year of Open Admissions) we had moved from no testing to two days of testing for many students, one day for the general tests and one for the specialized tests. Since the general tests now took the whole day, fatigue had to be considered, although we did not have any way of judging its impact on test results. We tried scheduling certain tests—such as reading—first, when students were likely to be fresh, but we did not formally evaluate the effect of test order on results. Testing experts have no doubt done this, but in the absence of test experts, we relied on our best judgment.

Other problems were encountered. We were new at testing and did not have a college testing office. The choice of tests, proper administration of them, hiring and training of proctors, and follow-through with the computer center on scoring programs and statistical analysis of results all had to be done by faculty and administrators who had many other demands on their time. Administratively and educationally, this is not a good way to run an important testing program, but it was the only way we could respond to the situation in which we found ourselves. We were also dealing with the remnants of the original college response to Open Admissions—a distrust of standardized testing and a belief that students should be offered the opportunity to participate in decisions about their first-semester course choices. The test scores, then, were still considered somewhat advisory; academic advisers could use discretion in overruling test results.

In the summer of 1972, for the first time, we scheduled an additional testing session in July to service students who for various reasons had missed the first session. The English department tried eliminating the essay for these students in order to shorten the testing time and to see if placements could be made solely on the basis of an objective test. The department found that the objective test was fine for gross sorting—"needs remediation" or "does not"—but only a writing sample can indicate the fine distinctions between levels of remediation or the need for ESL (English as a Second Language) placement. In fact, the objective test originally adopted to select for ESL problems could not discriminate ESL from among a variety of other nonstandard English problems such as dialect and black English; when used without a writing sample, the test often indicated ESL placement for students who spoke only English.

Remedial courses and placement tests were here to stay. In 1972-73 we joined forces with the SEEK program (Search for Education, Elevation, and Knowledge), which had been testing and requiring remediation since its establishment at Hunter in 1969, to agree on a common battery of tests for the entire freshman class. No decision about tests is going to be liked by all. There are things wrong with each of the tests we adopted and each we rejected. There are supporters and detractors of the ones we use and of those we do not use. Some of those we use work well for certain of our students but do not tell us much about others. In short, no battery of tests is perfect.

There were several options open to us, all of which we explored. One was to use a complete national battery, such as the SAT or ACT (American College Testing). Neither of these seemed to us to discriminate at the lower end of the spectrum, which is where we need to make distinctions for remedial course levels. Another option, and probably the best in the long run, was to develop our own tests tailored to our student body and curriculum, but this is both time consuming and expensive. We did not have the experts on our staff to do it, nor could we wait. We needed tests by the spring for the next group of September entrants. So we compromised and took the only other avenue open to us: we chose a combination of tests that SEEK had found helpful and those that our remedial departments favored.

Our battery now includes objective tests for the three skills—reading, written English, and mathematics—plus an essay and the second-language test, now used mostly for reading placements. We decided that whether or not the tests were liked by all, we would stick with them long enough to obtain comparative data. (Because of the many test changes made in the first three years, we cannot compare the performance of those early classes either with each other or with later classes, thus thwarting research and evaluation efforts.) The use of a variety of tests from different manufacturers presented an unforeseen problem, that of designing a single machine-scoreable answer sheet that could accommodate all of the tests. Otherwise, administration of the tests to as many as 1,200 students at a time with several answer sheets per student would have been a nightmare.

Once we decided upon the test battery, we set dates for a major testing in the spring, a backup in July for late acceptances, and a final cleanup session at the end of August, sufficiently before the late registration period (just before the beginning of classes), to give us test results, but late enough to catch all the stragglers. All students, both SEEK and non-SEEK, would be required to attend one of these sessions in order to register. We tried making some exceptions, exacting a promise from the excepted students to come to a session during the semester; but we have found that the students do not come and that we are back to our old guessing game about where to place them in courses. The "no test, no registration" policy is therefore applied without exception.

On May 22, 1973, the Hunter College Senate doubled our work by a single resolution: it mandated that *all* Hunter students demonstrate minimum proficiency in written English, reading, and mathematics by passing either tests or appropriate courses at Hunter. The reasons for this lay in the CUNY transfer policies.

The Open Admissions plan originally provided for free transfer of A.A. (Associate in Arts) and A.S. (Associate in Science) degree holders from CUNY community colleges to the senior colleges. As liberal arts degrees, these associate degrees required approximately the same course work as our students took during their first two years, and we could all agree that they were transferable. Many of the community colleges also offered technical and career programs for which they awarded the A.A.S. (Associate in Applied Science) degree; a few of these programs were formally articulated with complementary degree programs in the senior colleges (for example, accounting and nursing), but in general the A.A.S. had been contemplated as a terminal degree. In the spring of 1973 the Board of Higher Education decided that all A.A.S. degree holders— students who had set their sights on technical careers— should be given the freedom to broaden their horizons and change their minds so that they could work for the B.A. degree. Commendable as it was, the practical effect of this policy was that another large group of students would be coming to Hunter with preparation quite different from the liberal arts preparation of our own students. We needed some way of assessing the new students' skill levels and preparation in order to place them in appropriate Hunter courses.

With this newest category of transfer students, the problem was the nature of the courses presented for transfer; in the past only liberal arts courses were recognized in determining eligibility, but many of the A.A.S. programs required few liberal arts credits. A student who had had two years of automotive technology, for example, could not come to Hunter and expect to enter advanced physics courses.

This new problem reinforced our decision that testing become a requirement for registration. During the summer of 1973, therefore, we tested almost 3,000 transfer students, telling them in June that, although they had already been notified of their acceptance, they would now have to take tests in July or August before they could register. As with any new policy instituted late in the sequence of events without adequate advance planning, we were not completely successful in carrying it out. The bulk of the testing had to be scheduled when staff was at a minimum, so that decisions and exceptions were difficult to make. We could not recruit enough proctors on such short notice, since many of the students were either away or already had summer jobs and plans. The testing therefore had to be done en masse in the auditorium, using lap boards for desks and a public address system for giving instructions and answering questions. We could be sure that the same directions were given to all test takers, but otherwise the situation was confusing, chaotic, and far from ideal.

This new regulation also put us in an awkward position. Students coming from colleges outside the CUNY system were insulted by our testing requirements; students from within CUNY believed that since we were all part of the same system Hunter should not put this additional burden on them. Yet Hunter could not put itself in the position of judging other colleges, saying that courses from one college would satisfy math proficiency, for example, whereas the same courses from another college would not. Our only resort was to test everybody. The only exceptions were for previously nonmatriculated students in our own School of General Studies who had been accepted for matriculation. Since the senate regulation specified that proficiency could be satisfied either by tests or by passing appropriate courses at Hunter, we were able to exempt these nonmatrics from certain tests, depending upon the courses they had taken at Hunter. Not having been able to anticipate this wrinkle in advance, we had to develop procedures for handling it as we went along, thus undoubtedly excluding some students who should have been considered for exemptions. Working out guidelines for exceptions and keeping adequate records of them presented problems that summer, although they have now become part of our regular functioning.

If there was one thing we learned that summer, it was that adequate lead time for planning how to implement new policies is essential for the smooth and effective inauguration of those policies. Unfortunately, almost every decision associated with Open Admissions at Hunter, and at the City University as well, has been made at the last minute and has therefore necessitated emergency actions for its initiation.

Settling into this new testing requirement and refining procedures became the order of business in 1974-75. Administratively, we were able to plan for testing dates at least a year in advance and to work with the admissions office in getting decisions made early enough for testing requirements and dates to be announced to all incoming students so they could make plans in advance. We also were able to work with the Computer Center to develop regular scoring programs and avoid emergency foul-ups. Internally, we could begin to catch up on all of the exceptions and work out procedures for avoiding them in the future.

Improvement of test administration was given a boost when a part-time test coordinator was hired. We could all start working toward needed improvements. The Office of Academic Advising, for example, was not pleased with the large group-advising session in the morning before the tests; students were anxious to get on with tests rather than listen to a series of speakers on unfamiliar topics. Some of the upperclassmen whom we had consulted about how to humanize testing had suggested that we begin the tests as soon as possible and delay the academic advising until later in the day. We therefore experimented in December and January with bringing in the whole staff of academic advisers to speak to students in the classrooms in between tests about what they should do to prepare for their first registration at Hunter. We found this extremely successful. Since the students knew something about what the tests were like, they could listen to the advisers with better attention; since they were in classrooms with no more than thirty students, they were more likely to ask questions and get their problems resolved. This also eliminated the problem we used to have of getting about 1,000 students from the auditorium to the classrooms on the upper floors when only one or perhaps two elevator operators were on duty Saturday and Sunday (and it was not economical to bring extra help in for the half-hour of the big crush). Scheduling the twelve to fifteen advisers to visit thirty to thirty-five rooms has presented a logistics problem, but we have been able to work it out with cooperation from the testing coordinator.

Handling large numbers of students in a high-rise building requires detailed plans made well in advance. Confusion and chaos can affect the test results as much as can bad instructions, so that a smoothly running test situation is essential. We have found that we should know all of the possible types of students expected (for example, on cleanup dates we have both freshmen and transfer students coming for tests), and there should be several persons in the lobby to direct students to the testing rooms or to holding areas for further directions. The shortage of elevators requires that some students walk to the lower floors while others are taken to upper floors in the elevator that is in service. Proctors must know their room assignments and have their rooms set up well in advance of the time the test is to begin. Materials must be counted out and ready for the proctors to pick up, which means that there must be specified hall stations where proctors report. At Hunter there may be three or four widely separated floors on which testing rooms are located, although we try to limit the room clusters to two or three floors if we can get enough rooms; this means that we have at least two hall stations, three if necessary. There must be roaming proctors for each floor who can relieve room proctors, relay room readiness to the reception area, be consulted by room proctors who encounter problems, deliver messages or changes in procedures during the testing, keep track of times when rooms are ready for advisers, lunch, etc., and in general assist the floor manager in keeping things running smoothly and act as a communication channel with other floors. Extra proctors—for running errands between floors, for alphabetizing essays, and even for erasing answer booklets when tests must be reused the next day—are also needed. In other words, personnel needs must be carefully considered, for they are large and crucial.

Communication is another essential. Walkie-talkies borrowed from our security office have at last resolved this problem. Provisions must also be made for special problems. Handicapped students may need a different room and even an individual proctor if financing allows that luxury. Ways of dealing with ill students must be anticipated, and decisions as to when to turn away late stragglers must be agreed upon by all. Someone must be around to answer the myriad questions that can be posed by 1,000 students who are unfamiliar with the college. Professional test administrators know all of these things, but those of us who backed into testing had to learn by doing, by trial and error.

The big problem that still has not been licked is the training of proctors. At registration the advisers would hear complaints from the new students that proctors had told them "not to worry about the tests, they don't mean anything," on the one hand, or warnings on the other hand that "you better do well on the tests or you'll get kicked out." It is obvious that the reliability of the test results is only as good as the testing situation. Without adequate proctor training there was no telling what went on in those rooms. For example, incorrectly filled out answer sheets present terrible problems with machine-scoreable tests. Untrained proctors are not aware of this seemingly unimportant but crucial point, and only training will impress the point on them. If a student's name and social security number are incorrectly entered on the answer sheet, it is hard to believe that the rest of the areas have been marked correctly. And if the answers have not been recorded correctly, the results are useless. The proctors are our only way of supervising this.

Once the testing coordinator was hired, she began immediately to increase proctor training, but there were limits to what she could demand in the way of volunteer time from them (proctors are paid during the tests but not for training time). The Office of Academic Advising cooperated with her during the fall of 1975 in developing a training videotape and in helping recruit students. There is still the problem, however, of undergraduate students not seeing themselves as authority figures and of being too close to the testing situation to function "on the other side of the desk." It is hard enough for an experienced teacher to take over a new class and develop any rapport with it in a single day; it is doubly difficult for an untrained undergraduate. We hope to be able to work with the education department in getting some of their graduate students to work with us on perfecting the testing procedures as part of their course work in testing and measurement. Helping with the various phases of our testing program would give these students valuable field experience and would contribute to the college at the same time. Proctoring would help them understand the physical demands of the job, the problems of misunderstood directions and test anxiety, and the nature of the emergencies that can arise. They could help with proctor training and also with the organization of the whole operation. They would bring a professional commitment to these activities that cannot be expected of undergraduates, and they could therefore expand the supervisory influence of the test administrator by acting as an extra link between her and the undergraduate proctors.

In a different vein, another problem that the remedial departments have been confronted with all along has been the strong feeling on the part of some students that the test results are not true indications of their abilities and that they should not be placed in remedial courses. We have to pay some attention to this, for it is hard to know what state a student was in on the testing day and how that state might have affected the results. In addition, the score on a particular test is but a single measure of the student's performance and might not be at all indicative of the student's general performance level. There is always an element of chance in a particular test score, as evidenced by the standard error of measurement factor. The student should be given the benefit of the doubt, if at all possible.

The Developmental English Program believes this is particularly true with respect to reading, since reading comprises many skills and is hard to measure with a single test. Since 1974, therefore, the Developmental English Program has been routinely scheduling a second test for all students scheduled into reading remediation to give them a chance to test up or out. When possible, the retest is scheduled prior to registration so that reassignments during the first week of class can be kept to a minimum. Students who cannot come in for the first retest, however, are retested during the first week of class to give them the same second chance as their classmates.

On the other hand, there is no organized attempt to retest for writing placement before registration, since the remedial placement decisions in this area are based on several pieces of evidence—the objective tests and the writing sample, which is read by at least two faculty members and by a third if necessary to resolve differences of opinion. Furthermore, one of the first in-class assignments is a writing sample; if the instructor spots an obvious mistake at that time, the student can still be reassigned immediately.

Retesting procedures are somewhat different for the two mathematics remedial courses. Students are given the opportunity of a retest for both at registration. The coordinator of the lower-level course in arithmetic has devised a ten-item test that, unlike the original test, is not timed and may ease the students' apprehension; it covers the subject matter of the course, and if passed, exempts a student on the spot. The coordinator of the upper-level course allows students so wishing to take the final examination of the course; they may look at the text first to see if they think they know the material. This test may be taken both by students who have just exempted themselves out of the arithmetic course and by those who were placed directly into the upper-level remedial course by the placement tests. Interestingly enough, fewer students dispute placement into the mathematics remedial courses than into the reading courses, probably because math competence is fairly concrete and obvious. Also, it is easier in our society to admit weakness in math than in reading. But mistakes can be made, and means should be provided for taking this possibility into account. It is just as bad to make students sit through a semester of remediation when they do not need it as to deny it when it is needed. The purpose of the tests is not to fill up remedial courses but to find the most rational and consistent means possible for identifying skill levels.

In Summary

Choosing tests is only one part of testing students for skill levels. Although everyone may not agree that skills can be determined by standardized tests, at the same time there does not now seem to be a better or fairer way of finding out about students' skill levels, especially when large numbers are involved. We certainly found at Hunter that placing students in courses on the basis of high school grade-point averages, or offering them the opportunity to assess their own skill levels and decide on their own place-ment, did not work. Tests, on the basis of which all of the entering students could be compared with each other with some degree of consistency, seemed to be the only equitable way of making such decisions. Otherwise, we were put in the position of making judgments about other schools that we were not equipped to make or of relying on students' self-perceptions, perceptions that may be un-realistic or may reflect unrealistic assessments in their former schools.

Once the decision to rely on testing is made, however, means for reassessing the test results, when the situation seems to suggest it, must be provided. All students have a bad day now and again, for example. Sometimes there are external circumstances during the testing period, such as a fire across the street, that can affect the results negatively. With machine-scored answer sheets the possibility of inad-vertently filling in the answer bubbles in the wrong se-quence, and thus throwing the whole test off, exists. Some skills are harder to measure than others and may therefore warrant routine retesting, as with reading. We have no way of knowing how long it has been since some of our entering students have taken arithmetic; this should not affect the results, but it may in some cases. And although many test experts say that time tests are accurate, some stu-dents simply do not work well in pressure situations; they should be given the chance to prove themselves, or alter-natively, to convince themselves that they do indeed need remediation.

We have found that proctors are a critical part of the test-ing operation and that their activities cannot be left to chance. They can be important factors in explaining the purpose and seriousness of the tests to the entering students, many of whom are quite unsophisticated about test taking, and they can provide a supportive atmosphere and be helpful in relieving the anxiety of the test takers.

Their attitude is transmitted to the students and should exert a positive force during a difficult day. In addition, the care with which they give instructions, answer questions, and check the answer sheets affects the technical quality of the answers and also eases the burden of the test coordinator in later having to correct sheets and supply missing information. The knowledge that instructions have been carefully given and problems watched for during tests supports our reliance on test results as valid indicators of the students' probable performance levels.

Finally, the organization of the testing sessions must be carefully planned, which implies that there should be one person who has full-time responsibility for coordinating all testing and for assessing the effectiveness of the procedures and of the tests themselves. When there are 1,000 or more students coming in at a specified time, preparations must be detailed and made well in advance. There must be plenty of people on hand to deal with the students, and all of the people involved must have common understandings of each other's functions and of their own individual responsibilities. Methods of communication, especially in spread-out situations, must be flexible, fast, and reliable. It takes time to ensure that all of these activities are going to run smoothly.

Perhaps these conclusions seem self-evident to anyone who has been actively involved in mass testing procedures, but for those of us who had had no more experience than giving exams in our classes and who did not have the resources of a college testing office, these lessons were learned the hard way. Until you have been through it, it is difficult to foresee all of the problems, but the more attention that is paid to detail, the smoother the testing day will be and the more confident you can be that the results are reliable—and the easier it will be on everybody involved, both the students taking the tests and those who are giving them.

6 Preregistration and Registration Advising

Registration is a perpetual problem at all large colleges. This is especially true during the registration of new students, who need a wide range of information to be able to make program decisions intelligently. Some schools bring in all of their new students a week before the semester begins, to introduce them to the college and its programs; others schedule a weekend retreat; some rely on distribution of written materials. Most assume that their entering students have a reasonable idea of what college is and what they want to take during their first term. Indeed, Hunter used to operate under this assumption.

Strict entrance requirements at Hunter meant that the preparation of most students was fairly uniform and that only those who planned ahead for college were there, often sure of their main interest. Hence, there was one day for orientation by upperclassmen (sometimes carried out on a weekend retreat), and there was one day for registration, called Arena Registration since it was organized like a big circus. The faculty were seated at tables around the perimeter of the gymnasium with lists of the available seats in the various courses. Students would stand

69

in line at the appropriate departments to reserve seats for enough courses to fill out their schedules. Before 1970, when the entering class was about half the size that it is now, this system provided some opportunity for faculty members to talk to individual students, and persuasive students could plead their cases for seats in closed courses. Because of the crowds, there was no time for real advising, but advising was considered unnecessary anyway. The curriculum for the first two years was fairly rigid, offering few choices to the incoming students: for example, to take music or art appreciation, to continue a language studied in high school or start a new one. It was assumed that the freshmen had no other questions. No one knew whether or not they experienced any disappointments, nor did we have time to find out. Somehow the day ended, and classes began the following week.

The Committee on Open Admissions, however, recognized that this situation was inadequate for a student body with a different background. Efforts were therefore made in the summer of 1970 to provide academic advice to at least the students with a high school average below eighty, who were defined as Open Admissions students. These students were called in for appointments with a group of graduate students who were specifically hired and trained to help them with program planning. The students with high school averages above eighty were sent materials and asked to return a program plan for review; if the advisers had questions, the students were asked to come in to discuss the proposed programs.

All this seemed to be working well until the day for Arena Registration arrived. The new freshmen took their approved plans to the gymnasium, and, along with the new transfer students, tried to sign up for classes—only to find that many of them were already full. There were no counselors to help with alternate plans; the faculty advisers had no idea about how or why program decisions had been made, so could offer little assistance; and the registrar's staff knew only registration procedures. The freshmen ended up in classes, but their programs often bore no resemblance to the plans so carefully made in the summer. Some students found themselves in advanced-level courses simply because those courses happened to meet at a particular hour on a given day and could be substituted for an introductory-level course meeting at the same time. The freshmen, unfamiliar with the subject of anthropology, for instance, had no idea that Culture and Personality must be preceded by Introduction to Cultural Anthropology, and in the press of registration they did not know how to use the *Bulletin* to find this out. The faculty advisers, unaware of whether requests were from freshmen or upperclassmen, did not have the time to ask about prerequisites. It was only after reports came back from the classroom later in the semester, and after a large number of students requested permission to drop courses when midterm test results showed that they were doing poorly, that the administration became aware of how serious the problem was.

Before Registration

At that point plans were made to revamp the process of preparing new freshmen for their first semester at college. As soon as we received our allocation of September entrants, the students were asked to report for tests in combination with a preregistration advising session to be held in the college auditorium. The newly appointed coordinator of freshman programs, along with the dean of students and a few other officials, greeted the students and gave them copies of the *Bulletin* and a pamphlet entitled "What Every Freshman Should Know." The coordinator discussed aspects of the Hunter curriculum that the students should think about in making their preliminary course choices, and also invited them to participate in

Conference Days. After a question and answer period, students were sent to the testing rooms for an afternoon of English tests.

At Conference Days (two days in late May), representatives from each of the departments and programs gathered in the gymnasium to answer questions about courses and majors. Since offices are scattered all over the college and office hours vary, Conference Days were the most efficient way for the students to be able to meet faculty without calling and coming to the school numerous times. The sessions were also necessary because registration was planned for the month of June, when few, if any, faculty members are at the college; questions that were not answered before June would remain unanswered. The preregistration advising and Conference Days gave students an opportunity for personal consultations to help them prepare for registration.

Initial Registration

Registration itself was also reorganized. Five academic advisers were recruited, each to head a team of three upperclassmen who were hired as schedulers. Each advising team would see six students an hour in the gymnasium; after the adviser discussed and approved program plans, the schedulers would work out the actual days and hours for class attendance. Once the schedules were completed, the freshmen would go to the other end of the gym, where the registrar's personnel could check them into classes immediately; if sections were closed, the freshmen could return to their group for rescheduling. Presumably, rescheduling could be kept to a minimum, for as sections closed, the information could be circulated to all the schedulers.

This system was certainly much better than the nonsystem of the year before; most students completed registration in two to three hours without major catastrophes and had a chance to talk with both an adviser and some upperclassmen. It was not ideal, however. It was very inefficient since every schedule was prepared individually by an upperclassman—while the freshman watched. Most students did not understand the process of actually making out a schedule, a handicap when they had to register for the following semester's classes by themselves. That first spring it took three weeks to register about 1,800 students. Although we planned to start at 9:30 and finish by 4:30 in the afternoon, there were few days when we were able to meet that schedule, even though we worked through lunch. Such pressure is bearable for the first go-round, but it cannot be tolerated year after year.

In subsequent semesters, therefore, we hired more student schedulers to speed up the process, and also recruited additional part-time advisers to give the full-time people some relief; nonstop advising is exhausting, especially when it lasts three full weeks. We also moved toward registering students in special programs (e.g., nursing) on different days, so that our advisers and those special program advisers could ensure that their particular sequences were properly planned. During the first two years we also scheduled first the students with high school averages below eighty, under the assumption that they had the greatest limitations on course selections and should have the greater number of open sections available in those courses that they could handle. Later, when we moved toward testing as the criteria for course planning, we gave out registration appointments (except for nurses) on a random basis.

In January 1973, the gymnasium was not available during intersession. This proved fortuitous, for we moved to the Reference Room of the library for registration. The library room was large, but at least it was not as cold and inhospitable as the gymnasium, and there were already large tables and chairs that could be used for our advising groups. In the library we were able to set up portable blackboards on which we could record closed sections as they filled up, thus eliminating some unnecessary returns for rescheduling. The visual record was an improvement over the runners we had used in the gym, but still did not solve this difficult problem. Often the schedulers found it easier to go directly to the registrar's table themselves and check sections, a solution that added to the time required for each student. Despite the more pleasant surroundings, there was still a feeling of mass numbers and confusion because about 150 to 200 students, schedulers, advisers, and registrar's staff were all in the library at any given time.

A difficulty with this registration process, no matter where it took place, was an inefficient use of time. At the beginning of the day, the advisers were busy seeing students to get them ready for scheduling, but the schedulers were idle. Toward the end of the day, the advisers were through and wanted to leave, while the schedulers had a backlog of students; but if the advisers left, there was no one to suggest substitutions if all available sections of a programmed course were filled.

Again, an external factor provided us with a solution. In January 1975, the Reference Room was being renovated; the alternate space offered us was too small for comfort, and the gymnasium was not available. We had to be content with a suite of seven contiguous classrooms. This gave us a chance to experiment with a new model for registration: group advising, conducted in a classroom of thirty students. The plan was that once the classroom was filled an adviser would take about thirty to forty-five minutes to interpret the test results given to the students when they arrived, discuss the alternatives open to students on the basis of those test results, and explain how to plan a schedule and fill out the registration forms. Instructions were given in the use of the *Schedule of Classes, Closed Section List,* and other materials that students would have to use in all future registrations. Assisting the adviser in the classroom were five upperclass "peer advisers" who had been given about fifteen hours of special training in working with groups, in interviewing and listening skills, and in college rules and regulations. These peer advisers helped students make choices about courses and then supervised them as they worked out schedules and filled out the necessary forms. The academic adviser circulated from small group to small group, talking individually with each freshman and finally approving each program; in addition, the adviser was able to spend time with the problem cases and refer special problems to the registration coordinator.

Two rooms were set up along these lines, one for students who required no remediation at all, and the other for those who required some remediation. The remaining rooms were set up in our normal fashion—one adviser with five schedulers who prepared schedules after the adviser decided on the program with each new student. An additional room in the suite was reserved for problems, which might range from handicapped students who needed individual attention, to students who were pro-testing test results or whose test results could not be found, to any other kind of exception that is bound to occur when 1,800 people are involved. We also had one room in which retesting in math and testing for calculus readiness were taking place.

The success of two aspects of this setup was apparent almost immediately. First, the group-advising model was far superior to the old adviser-scheduler patterns. Students were registered more quickly; the students themselves felt that they received more personal attention, had greater freedom in decision making, and were more confident when regular registration for the next semester came up; and many more students could be registered during a given period of time. In fact, we registered half again as many students as before in the same amount of time with fewer people doing scheduling and advising. Second, the use of classrooms rather than one big hall cut down on the feeling of chaos and of being overwhelmed by large numbers of people. The reception area was crowded during the first half-hour of the morning or afternoon, when 150 students reported there. But as soon as the students were assigned to classrooms, the area seemed deserted, although students moved from classrooms to the retesting area or to the registrar's area or to the problem room, and the runner moved among rooms posting closed sections on the blackboards, where they could be kept in numerical order and therefore be more readable.

We now use the group-advising model exclusively for registration of all new students, both freshmen and transfer students, but we have made several refinements. Classroom assignments are made to achieve homogeneity; one classroom for students requiring no remedial courses, another for those requiring only some form of mathematics help, another for students who are deficient in English skills, either reading or writing or both, and another for those needing all types of remediation. When all of the students in a given classroom have the same problem, the advising is much easier. And the fact that all of the students in the room are in the same boat is reassuring to those involved. We have found that we need more support personnel in the rooms where students require all three forms of remediation, while the rooms for students with no remedial requirements can operate with a minimum of personnel and finish more quickly. Thus, we can assign students and professional advising personnel where they are needed most, and reassign them to slow rooms as the period draws to a close to help clear up the problems of slow decision makers. As mentioned above, we can also keep up with the closed sections much more efficiently, cutting down on the number of return trips from the registration area for rescheduling. Providing mathematics and calculus testing on the spot reduces the number of misplacements that have to be corrected during the first week of classes. Most important, however, is the feedback from the students involved, which indicates that their first registration was not a complete trauma. Naturally, some of the students are not going to be pleased with their programs and are going to be confused by the newness of the process, but these problems are at a minimum, if our complaint calls and comments during the semester are any indication.

If we move toward computerized registration at terminals, we can still use a modification of this system, because it is primarily based on providing information to the students at appropriate times prior to their beginning classes and on keeping all contacts as personal as possible. We start with the bare minimum of information—a *Bulletin* and the distillation of program-planning hints in "What Every Freshman Should Know"—dispensed in small group sessions on the testing date; an opportunity to explore specific interests in more depth with faculty advisers on Conference Days; and finally, a fairly relaxed registration day on which we attempt to provide maximum opportunities for contacts with both advisers and students as well as experience with the forms that students will have to use for all subsequent registrations. Our intention is that all of this occur in a supportive environment, but no longer do we do everything for students as in former days; we found that this crippled them in later dealings with the system.

It is also important to have the registrar's staff working closely with the advising personnel. Only in this way can realistic advising take place; the best advising in the world is useless if the programs are not possible because of closed sections or sections that are available only at times that are not convenient for the students. In fact, after a few days many of the schedulers are so familiar with the open courses that they can suggest appropriate classes for particular times during the day or for certain days of the week. Such two-way communication, which certainly will be improved by moving to an on-line computerized system, is a vital component of good registration advising for the new students.

After Registration

Once the new students are registered, concern with their program is by no means over. For one thing, initial registration for the new students takes place between two weeks (for the February semester) and two months (for the September semester) before school starts. Many things can happen in these periods that may require students to change their programs, such as taking summer courses, retesting for remedial courses after registration, a new job, changes in family responsibilities, and so forth. Students may also decide after attending their first class that a particular course is not for them. Hence, we know that there will be changes made during the first week of school, which is the official "add-drop" week at Hunter.

We expected that many students would attempt to drop remedial courses or add courses for which they were patently unprepared, if they did not agree with some of the test results. If the college had gone to the expense and trouble to test students and provide an elaborate and personalized advising and registration process prior to the beginning of school, we could not let it all go down the drain during the first week of school for lack of foresight.

We therefore arranged with the registrar during that first fall of 1971 to see to it that all changes of program initiated by freshmen had to have Academic Advising approval.

Initially, this meant intolerable long lines in front of the advising office, as well as the confusion within the office of sorting out students who had problems not associated with program changes. It was obvious that we had to work out new procedures for approving these changes, without overburdening both the students and our small staff. Our final solution was that academic advisers are assigned to the registrar's area during the first week of classes, and that all students who are in remedial courses or are freshmen must secure Academic Advising approval before turning in their paperwork to the registrar.

It may seem strange to have to even mention this, since in many colleges all program changes must have an adviser's approval, but Hunter has always had a very permissive registration system. With the exception of certain divisions such as nursing, or health sciences and education, no student has had to have any approval to select a course. Academic Advising, therefore, had to institute a policing action that went against the grain of tradition. Many faculty members are still not aware of this requirement, and some students resent it. Our problem may be unique to Hunter, but the principle is valid nevertheless; if it is important to approve initial programs, it is equally important to scrutinize any changes made in those programs, either during the official add-drop period or during the rest of the semester. The incorporation of such restrictions into an ongoing permissive system is difficult; but it is not impossible, once one realizes that it is a matter of communicating and coordinating with numerous other offices to make sure they understand the procedural changes. In other words, it becomes a problem of bureaucratic change, as well as one of academic-advising constraints.

What has been said about program changes also applies to subsequent program planning and registration and is especially crucial for students who are in remedial courses.

If remedial sequences are indeed necessary, then students' progress through them must be monitored. Prescriptions against taking certain courses while in remedial courses—for example, no science courses for students requiring mathematics remediation—must also be enforced. Again, the Office of Academic Advising had to find ways of accomplishing these ends with a limited staff. We tried requiring all students in remedial courses to pick up their registration materials in the advising office, in the hope that they would automatically see an adviser to plan their programs when coming in for their materials. Several things were wrong with this assumption. Students came in at times that were convenient for them, not necessarily when we had plenty of advisers in the office. We could not keep sufficient staff on hand to take care of peak periods, nor could we neglect the other students who needed appointments for other problems. And some students found ways to "beat the system" and somehow procure their registration materials without ever setting foot in the advising office.

We tried several methods for improving our monitoring activities. First, we instituted midterm grades, which we then brought to registration (for spring classes, registration took place during the last six weeks of the fall term) where we tried to look up grades for each freshman as an aid in program planning. This did not work. Perhaps in other colleges it might, but at Hunter, since there are almost no classes that are exclusively for freshmen, many instructors did not give midterm exams in time to get grades processed through the system prior to registration. After trying to improve the system for a few semesters, we finally abandoned it. In the meantime, we inaugurated the system of stationing academic advisers in the registration area during the entire registration period to approve programs as required. The "as required" component was systematically developed over time as other changes took place. It started with scrutinizing freshman programs, then approving freshmen on Academic Stop (i.e., in remedial courses), and finally approving all students—both freshmen and transfer students—who are in any part of the remedial sequence and therefore on Academic Alert (the successor to Academic Stop). The registration materials of these students are specially stamped, and a letter is sent to them indicating the steps they should take to register, including the remedial sequence they must follow and the need for consultation with an academic adviser before final approval of their registration each semester until they complete the remedial courses required for them. In the absence of a mandatory advising system, this seems to be the most manageable way of overseeing a remedial structure and of avoiding some of the grossest problems arising from self-advising on the part of students who do not have realistic perceptions of their skills in relation to the courses they wish to take. We realize that some students may be unfairly (i.e., unnecessarily) monitored by this policing system, but the advisers are always on the lookout for such exceptions so that we can deal with them as anomalies.

An important aspect of this change in Hunter's traditional approach to registration is the realization that registration is not just a mechanical action but rather a decision-making process that has implications for the student both in the next semester and in the long range of that student's career and life goals. As mentioned before, prior to 1970 few choices were required of students during their first two years because of fairly rigid basic liberal arts course requirements. When these requirements were relaxed, many more decisions had to be made, and the students were not always equipped to make them. Academic Advising was set up to try to deal with the problems, but it also had a new function in an ongoing bureaucracy and had to feel its way cautiously and slowly. Advising still is not mandatory at Hunter for every student, which means that students who are not in remediation can fall through the cracks, and no one is really to blame—except the college, which does not require them to get advice.

Training of Personnel

Because registration is such a crucial process for both the students and the college, it cannot be left to chance. Not only must the process be carefully monitored, but the people involved in it must be properly trained. And this training must extend to both advisers and student assistants hired specifically for registration.

Training the advisers is somewhat the easier task of the two, since advisers are involved in assisting students all the time. Still, they must be reminded of important points unique to registration—for example, the significance of test scores, the prescriptions attached to certain remedial placements, the courses appropriate for students requiring heavy amounts of remediation versus the range of choices available to the excellent students, new majors and courses, special rules and regulations about registration that may not be called into question at any other time during the semester. All of these details can be brought together in a handbook and discussed at a briefing session—usually two hours—just prior to the registration period. This is a refresher course more than anything else, but it is absolutely essential; no matter how professional the staff is, they have other duties throughout the semester and tend to forget the special problems attached to registration. The session is also a good time to share problems and possible solutions.

Training of the student personnel is even more important for a successful registration. In 1971 we exposed the student schedulers to a couple of hours concerned with program planning, but assumed that they knew the college rules and regulations. We found that they often knew the myths of the rules and regulations and that one of the reasons for their own success was that they had learned how to deal with the bureaucracy—sometimes in unorthodox ways. This was not the kind of information we believed should be given to freshmen under official aegis. It was not that we objected to students telling other students how to make the system work for them; it was the inaccurate information that was being passed on that disturbed us. The importance of conducting training sessions became apparent for other reasons as well. The student schedulers were, after all, performing new behaviors in a new situation and they needed to know how to deal with the unfamiliar questions that were sure to arise.

We began by increasing the number of required training hours from two to four. In these additional hours we introduced role-playing sequences so that the schedulers could understand some of the anxieties of the new students and how best to deal with them. We also described the types of problems they could handle themselves and those that should be referred to the advisers. Of course, we could not possibly impart in four hours all the information and sensitivity necessary for what we now consider adequate performance in so vital an activity as registration. Until 1974-75 we did not have sufficient staff to do anything about this situation, since we had only one full-time staff member exclusively involved with registration and testing. It was only in September 1974, when we were able to hire three new full-time advisers, that we were able to devote concentrated attention to the problems that emerged as we gained experience with preregistration advising, testing, registration, and monitoring of the progress of remedial students through their first few semesters at Hunter. All of this is not to be taken either as an apology or as a defense, but rather as an affirmation of the importance of sufficient staff to do the kind of training that makes the difference between doing a job well and half doing it.

With the introduction of additional staff members, we have instituted a structured training program for the peer advisers who are an integral part of our registration system. These students are carefully interviewed and selected for their commitment to this kind of helping activity, their sensitivity to what others are saying by both words and actions, and for their ability to handle situations requiring innovative and mature responses. Staff members participate in the various phases of the training, which involves role-playing of types of students to be expected at registration, methods of dealing with various behavior patterns, techniques for working with small groups of students in helping with decision making, ability to assume authoritative roles in order to show new students how to fill out necessary paperwork, knowledge of appropriate rules, regulations, and policies, and understanding of when problems are of such magnitude that they should be referred to advisers.

This kind of training is expensive, but in the long run it is worth it for several reasons. It is invaluable, of course, for the students who go through it; this is the very kind of supervised experience that college can and should provide as preparation for future life activities. It enables us to service a large body of students efficiently and effectively and yet at a minimum cost. Finally, it develops a corps of students who can spread their influence to other students not only at registration but also throughout the year. In fact, it is so valuable that the Dean of Students' Office is now offering similar training as part of a course for peer counselors and has asked the Office of Academic Advising to cooperate in integrating academic advising instruction into the peer counseling training. One of the obviously positive outcomes of this entire experience will be the merging of the peer-counseling and the peer-advising training activities into one peer-training course. Such a course should develop a corps of undergraduates who can feed their expertise back into the college in all kinds of student-related service activities while at the same time gaining academic credit and valuable experience that will help them when they go out into the larger world looking for work.

In Summary

We have had to change our concepts about advising and registering new students in drastic ways since 1970. We have moved from stereotyping students according to their high school averages, which presumed academic performance, to judging them on the basis of competency as evidenced by performance on standardized tests. Although these tests are far from perfect, they are at least consistent, provided we can maintain the consistency of the testing situation and at the same time make allowances for individual differences.

We have been concerned with the dissemination of information to the new students, trying to give them only as much as they can handle at any given time and transmitting it in as personal a way as possible. We have also tried to do it in different ways—by personal contact in small groups, by opportunities to talk directly to faculty who are experts in given areas, by written materials, and by contacts with both advisers and peers. We have tried to minimize the mass nature of all these contacts, although we have to deal in large numbers because Hunter is a large, nonresidential school, populated by students who especially need to be treated as individuals.

We have come to recognize that such activities do not just happen. The people involved in them at all levels must be trained, aware of the problems that can arise, able to deal with them, and able to put themselves in the place of the new students who come to a new situation, often without a clue as to how to act and what is expected of them. We must be aware of the circumstance of the new students so that we can help them bridge the gap into college life in a positive way, starting from their very first experience with the institution.

7 Remedial Courses

Although we anticipated that Open Admissions students would be poorly prepared when they came to Hunter, we preferred to have them immediately enter into the main stream of the college rather than be separated from the rest of the student body. Consigning them to remedial courses was seen as somehow akin to relegating them to second-class citizenship. Instead, compensatory services were to be provided, built into the courses they took. Each department was to devise tutoring systems as part of or supplements to introductory courses. The hope was to bring the resources of the entire faculty to bear on the problem of the new students' academic deficiencies. This expectation, of course, assumed the agreement and cooperation of the total faculty, which hindsight tells us was unrealistic.

Even prior to Open Admissions, the English department had recognized that the single-semester composition course required for freshmen was insufficient for a number of entering students. An increase in underprepared students could only make this situation worse. Responding to the early adoption of the Open Admissions policy, the department created a course during the summer of 1970 to prepare such students for the conventional composition course. This new course was not considered to be remedial, and it carried three academic credits, although they did not fulfill the writing requirements for graduation. As a departmental effort, sorting students into the regular and preparatory classes had to be done during the regular class time, a serious but necessary interruption of instruction.

Important parts of the department's plan were the initiation of a tutoring service for students who needed more help than could be given in class and the provision for a "Y" grade in both courses to allow some students to take more than one semester to reach the exit criteria. As soon as classes started (about the fourth week in the term), the tutorial services were offered both to students who came in on their own and to students who were referred by their instructors. The tutorial staff also reviewed the test results of all students in an effort to persuade those who tested poorly to seek help. Records kept by the tutoring office indicated that about 10 percent of the students in the preparatory course and about 4 percent in the composition course actually utilized its services. A larger number of students were referred but never showed up, a problem often encountered when such services are optional. Unexpectedly, an unusually large proportion of students referred for tutoring exhibited second-language (ESL) problems. Evidently, weakness in English had a great deal to do with our students' difficulties in reading and writing. In the past, immigrant groups had evidently mastered English before applying for admission.

The first-semester patterns intensified in the spring semester. More students than before required tutoring in the composition course, reflecting continuing problems for those who had moved up from the lower-level course, and the proportion of tutored students with ESL problems increased.

As a result of its experiences during this first year, the English department modified the program in several ways. First, two hours of laboratory work were added to the three classroom hours of the preparatory course, and the emphasis of the course was changed from creative writing to development of reading comprehension skills as an underpinning for writing skills. Several reading specialists were hired for this purpose. Special sections in both courses were designated to handle ESL problems. Furthermore, as indicated in chapter 5, the tests were administered prior to registration so that valuable class time was not taken up with assigning students to the proper courses. There is always some provision for reassignment during the first week of class, based on in-class assessments by the instructors, but early testing was intended to keep this to a minimum.

Like the English department, the mathematics department had responded to the challenge of Open Admissions by developing a nonremedial college-level course that covered a wide range of topics. Entitled Basic Structures of Mathematics, it carried three academic credits that counted toward graduation and, unlike English, could also satisfy part of the Basic Prescription requirements in the sciences and mathematics area. The course was self-paced, taught in an audiovisual laboratory, and designed theoretically to serve students whose preparation ranged from no mathematics to three years of high school mathematics including some analytic geometry and some college algebra. It was anticipated that well-prepared students could complete the course in a semester or less, while those who came in with poorer backgrounds might spend longer periods of time on each unit and could make use of the "Y" grade.

Many problems were encountered with the course during the fall of 1970, the most serious of which was late delivery of equipment, so that the course was not able to function in the lab until December. In addition, the task of developing programmed-instruction materials took longer than anticipated, so that not all were ready when the equipment was installed. Many students became discouraged and dropped out during the term, although no one knows how many because of the confusion. These were problems brought on by the speed with which Open Admissions was put into effect; once things settled down in the second semester, the course ran smoothly and showed itself to be an efficient method of instruction.

Despite the evidence of Basic Structures of Mathematics, however, the instructors of science courses reported that many of their failing students could not deal with the content of the courses because they had not mastered the mathematics and the problem-solving techniques underlying the subject matter. This is not hard to understand after the fact, since the mathematics course did not even attempt to deal with these problems. It was not intended to make up for deficient backgrounds, but was primarily a course for students who were not planning to major in science or math but who wanted some exposure to the subject as part of a liberal arts education. Thus, the mathematics department had responded in an innovative way to what the Committee on Open Admissions had thought would be the needs of Open Admissions students to learn mathematics in a new way. The attempt, however, did not meet the real needs of these students when they sat in classes.

In fact, the college had no ways of providing this needed help, and the regular curriculum had other important purposes. The tutoring program was not set up to teach students skills they had never been exposed to; all it could do was fill in the gaps. Given Hunter's previous experience, these problems could not have been foreseen; they only surfaced as students actually sat through and, unfortunately, failed courses during the first year of Open Admissions.

The social sciences division and the humanities and arts division approached Open Admissions somewhat differently. Both concluded that there was no such thing as a "social science skill" or a "humanities skill" comparable to the "3 Rs," but realized at the same time that all three of these latter skills were required for students to be successful, especially in the many courses with heavy reading assignments. Several departments therefore cooperated with the spirit of the recommendations of the Committee on Open Admissions that new entry points be developed for Open Admissions students.

The sociology department, for example, set up a tutoring workshop that was staffed by graduate sociology students and was open several hours each day for freshmen to drop in and "discuss sociology," use textbooks that were donated by publishers, get help with assignments, and generally absorb the flavor of the discipline.

The psychology department redesigned its introductory course to provide for several freshman sections that were self-paced. Taught in large lecture sections, the course was divided into units with a list of questions covering the material in each unit given to the students. Each student was assigned to a coach, an upperclass psychology major responsible for about twelve freshmen. As the students mastered the material for each unit, they signed up for a quiz with their coach. The quizzes included both written and oral questions and were graded immediately; if not passed, they could be retaken without penalty. Because of its self-paced nature, this course also offered the "Y" grade for students who were not able to complete all of the units in one semester.

The urban affairs department developed a course in urban topics: students began with their own experiences, and through field work, specially selected readings, group discussions, and other directed activities, worked from the

concrete to the abstract. The theater and cinema department also created a new course in which students could
explore their own potential in the theater by experiential
means rather than through lectures and readings.

Despite these efforts, the feedback from all departments
was that students in a variety of courses were ill prepared
and that the problems were greater than individual
instructors could handle.

During the first semester of its existence, the experiences
of the Office of Academic Advising, which was established
in the second year of Open Admissions, tended to confirm
and enlarge upon the complaints heard from the departments. Among other things, the advisers found that high
school grades, which had been the major determinant for
course placement, were not always good indicators of
either skill levels or future performance. The quality of
education offered in the high schools ranged all the way
from excellent to poor. The programs taken by students
also varied widely. In New York City, for example, from
which the majority of Hunter's students come, there used
to be three types of diplomas—academic, commercial, and
general—and each had specific course requirements
appropriate to its purpose. In 1973 these were replaced by
a single general diploma, making it impossible for an
adviser to determine the type of preparation a student had
had. For example, three years of mathematics could
include algebra, trigonometry, and intermediate algebra;
or it could mean three years of bookkeeping. These
differences are crucial for students' abilities to handle
introductory science courses in college. Before Open
Admissions there were specific courses required for
admission; after 1970, however, the only requirement was
a high school diploma or its equivalent. The courses that
the students themselves had chosen therefore varied
considerably. Some students, never dreaming of entering

college, concentrated on nonacademic courses, which did them little good when they changed direction and decided to go to college. Others consciously chose the non-academic sessions of certain courses as an opportunity to make higher grades than their peers in the academic versions of the same courses, in order to ensure acceptance into the colleges that they chose. It is difficult to impress upon a high school student the long-range shortsightedness of such a choice, when the short-range results are more likely to bring immediate satisfaction.

The intuition of advisers likewise fails to be a good forecaster of how students will do in courses. Some students are highly articulate in verbal contacts, but are quite deficient in writing skills. Others learn almost entirely from listening in class, thus masking severe reading problems. These behaviors may enable a student to pass in high school and even function in many life situations, but will hinder college survival and may very well not show up in an advising interview.

In summary, it became apparent from the experiences of the academic departments and the Office of Academic Advising that the compensatory philosophy was not realistic, at least not for our commuting population. Motivation is not developed by osmosis, and underprepared students who sit in class do not take on college-student norms merely by physical contact. In fact, association with students who are obviously well prepared often so overwhelms the underprepared students that they turn off completely and develop a defeatist attitude. Necessary skills must be taught in structured situations that are part of a regularly scheduled program. We cannot expect students to make up on their own what they have not gotten in twelve prior years of school.

As mentioned above, the tutoring services of the English department were not fully utilized when attendance was voluntary. Academic Advising experienced the same phenomenon during the fall of 1971. Each student was urged to see an adviser to discuss programs, problems, and progress; about half made appointments to come in, and only half of those kept them. Many of the Open Admissions students did not know how to ask for help, or if they had at one time done so, had been callously treated and therefore discouraged from ever asking for it again. Also, defensiveness often precluded the admission that help should be sought. When, however, the help is considered normal, is required, and is provided in some sort of regular fashion with stated goals, then the possibility of its being used is greater. We all know how hard it is, for example, to make ourselves stick to a rigid diet on our own; to ask Open Admissions students to do this in areas where the probable rewards are not nearly as tangible as a svelte figure is unrealistic, to put it mildly.

Finally, most of the students coming to Hunter work some hours during the week. Once their class schedules have been determined, they plan their working hours and other activities, such as housework, socializing, and family responsibilities, around them. We found it optimistic to expect students to find additional time for extra hours of tutoring, especially when its value might be questionable in their eyes.

Although the college had not been able to foresee these problems, their seriousness was clear once a central office such as Academic Advising was able to look at the problem in an overall way. Feedback to the administration was of course an important function of the office. On its recommendation, therefore, a second Task Force on Open Admissions was appointed in the spring of 1972 to recommend how the college should respond to the new problems. Members of the task force not only looked at

Hunter's experiences but also investigated the literature about Open Admissions elsewhere and visited other CUNY colleges that had approached Open Admissions in a different fashion. On the basis of the evidence gathered, the task force recommended that remedial courses in reading, writing, and mathematics be instituted so that the content of regular courses would not be watered down, standards would not be lowered, and the academically well-prepared students would not be penalized. The task force also agreed that the poorly prepared students needed extra help with such things as study habits, note taking, test and exam taking, academic rules and regulations, decision making, program planning, and choice of major—in other words, some kind of freshman orientation seminar.

The English department, which had already become aware of many of these problems, proposed that reading and writing be dealt with separately and that writing remediation be further specialized into non-ESL and ESL programs. It was anticipated that students with writing problems would probably also read poorly, but it was intended that the system be flexible enough to allow for variations, such as the student who was concurrently in standard freshman composition and a remedial reading course.

The sciences and mathematics division responded by surveying all of the science departments, as well as several of the social science departments that require an understanding of mathematics in their curricula, to determine the concepts crucial for satisfactory completion of their introductory courses. Originally, a single semester of mathematics remediation had been contemplated, but the survey, together with the experiences in the previous two years, pointed toward a two-semester sequence that would go back far enough to make up for the arithmetic preparation some students had never reached. The division therefore recommended one course in Arithmetic and Topics in Algebra and a second course in Problem Solving in the Sciences. The latter was designed to build on the mathematical skills and apply them to problems fundamental to the natural and social sciences, such as averages, linear equations, areas and volumes, measurement tables, graphs, and charts. The purpose of the sequence was to develop the scientific literacy necessary for entry into the science and social science courses students would have to take later.

On the other hand, neither the social sciences division nor the humanities and arts division believed that remedial courses in their areas were appropriate. Rather, they agreed that ability to deal with their subject matter depended on proficiency in reading, writing, and mathematics and that students lacking these skills should not take their courses until the skills were mastered, just as science and English were off limits until related remediation was completed.

One additional course was developed, called the Freshman Seminar (see exhibit 1, which shows the course description distributed to students). Sponsored jointly by Academic Advising and the Office of Student Services (the new name for the Dean of Students' Office), its purpose was to take the students who were deemed the highest risks for failing—arbitrarily decided as those taking two or more remedial courses—and give them group advising for a semester. The purpose of the course was to make up for the kind of orientation to academic work that we assumed these students had never received in their previous schooling: to teach them study skills, to introduce them to decision making with respect to both time budgeting and course planning, to make them aware of their own responsibility for what happened to them either because of actions consciously taken or because of their own inaction or failure to learn rules and regulations. In the past, parents and friends had often performed this

Exhibit 1

ABOUT FRESHMAN SEMINAR

WELCOME TO FRESHMAN SEMINAR!

This is a one-credit course which meets one hour each week during your first semester at Hunter.

What will you learn in Freshman Seminar?

* * * * The Freshman Seminar is like a weekly guidebook to Hunter. You will get information which will help you to survive and succeed as a college student. You will find out about all the requirements and services of the College:

> Basic Prescription
> Majors and Minors
> Grading Systems
> Counseling and Advising Services
> Tutoring Services
> Student Activities
> Student Government

* * * * You will have an opportunity to discuss and get training in some of the skills necessary for college success:

> Note-Taking Skills
> Time-Management Skills
> Study Skills
> Test-Taking Skills
> Class-Participation Skills
> Decision-Making Skills

* * * * AND . . . you will be meeting with and getting to know a group of first-semester freshmen who are experiencing some of the same challenges, problems, and excitements as you are.

WELCOME TO FRESHMAN SEMINAR!

Note: Outline developed by Robert Cohn.

function for our students, but during our first semester in Academic Advising we found that many students were the first of their families, neighborhoods, and even extended circles who had considered college; they had no notion of what college was like and little cultural support that valued education for other than its advertised effectiveness in increasing lifetime earnings. The concept that a liberal arts education would make one a better person had no meaning to many of these students and was therefore not part of their goal structure. In fact, many factors were working against them, not the least of which were friends who were making good salaries without college and families who resented foregone earnings. Although the Freshman Seminar certainly could not perform social and psychological miracles, nor was it intended to, it could at least make the students aware of the realities of college life and academic planning.

All of these courses were suggested, planned, approved by the Hunter Senate, and put into the curriculum in that single spring 1972 semester, a miracle of academic change on a par with the initiation of Open Admissions; the difference that the remedial courses were not the result of administrative fiat but the outgrowth of an increasing realization that our original responses were not adequate and that the problem was more complicated than we had anticipated at the outset.

A major decision that credit would be given for these courses was made by those developing the remedial sequences, and was ultimately supported by both the administration and the Senate. The usual arguments were raised that college credit should not be given for subject matter that should have been learned in high school, on one side, and that we had to take students where they were and offer them some motivation for learning what they somehow had missed in the past, on the other side. The latter philosophy won out, and minimal credit is now granted for the remedial courses, although there is a limit to the total number of such credits that may be earned toward a degree. In addition, the Senate agreed that students could, if they wished at some later time, waive these credits so that they could take additional college-level courses. So far, only a few students have done this, but these exceptions support the contention that there may be latent talents in even the most unlikely students, talents that can be unlocked if opportunities are made available: in other words, the rationale for Open Admissions.

Tangible evidence of the motivational importance of credit was evident with the Freshman Seminar, which was the last remedial course to be considered by the Senate. All of the others had been approved at the Senate's last meeting in the spring of 1972, but the Freshman Seminar had been held over until the fall. The first several weeks of class were conducted without any certainty that credit would be approved or even that the course itself would be continued. During those few weeks attendance was irregular, and the instructors had no sanctions since an F in a no-credit course could have no effect on a student's average, the number of credits attempted and earned, or any of the other standards by which a student's performance is measured. Once the granting of a single credit was approved, attendance patterns changed dramatically. Students came back and missed few classes from then on; they also turned in the required papers and completed other assignments. In other words, the possibility of even a small reward made all the difference in the world in our ability to get students into class. This was, of course, especially important during the first semester when the course had no reputation; now, many students who are not required to take it sign up for it, since they have heard from friends that it is valuable—but the credit is still important to them.

The ways in which all of these remedial courses are structured varies according to the subject matter and department orientations. The one thing that is common is that they are all under the aegis of the academic departments, not isolated from the regular curriculum into a separate "skills" or "remedial" department. Within this context, each department has gone its own way.

Arithmetic and Topics in Algebra, for example, follows the self-paced model of the Basic Structures in Mathematics course, which is still in the curriculum. These two courses, as well as the introductory psychology course described earlier, use variations of what is known as the Keller Plan, or Personalized System of Instruction (PSI). PSI is based on the principle that students should be actively involved in their own learning and should have immediate reinforcement of this learning through quick feedback of test results at each level of skill mastery. Whereas the psychology course uses a large lecture and coaches, the math courses are taught in a Math Learning Center, or lab, and utilize a combination of audiovisual materials and written lessons along with self-tests, so that the student can proceed as slowly or quickly as mastery of the course material demands. When the student is ready, testing is done either by a paper-and-pencil test or at a computer terminal. The test is scored immediately by the tutor and the results discussed with the student; this discussion includes an analysis of weaknesses and suggestions for further study, when necessary. Under the Keller Plan one instructor is responsible for approximately 120 students and ten to twelve tutors, each of whom works directly with ten to twelve students. The tutors establish strong personal relationships with the students, since they take attendance, help with particular problems, score the tests, and discuss the results with the students. The instructor serves as an administrator and coordinator, reassigning tutors as necessary, answering tutors' questions, and in general overseeing the smooth operation of the course. Students are not kept to a rigid attendance schedule; by working at their own pace, many finish the course before the semester ends, enabling them to spend extra time on other courses, or possibly to go directly into the upper-level course if it is early in the semester. Other advantages of this mode are its flexibility, its almost infinite expandibility (depending on the availability of tutors), and its economy in comparison with regular instructional methods.

The Problem Solving in the Sciences course, on the other hand, was initially taught in the conventional lecture format. However, instructors covered the material in less than a semester, gave a final exam at the end of the eleventh week, and released those who passed the exam; those who did not pass reviewed the course materials and took a second final at the end of the semester. In both instances, all students were given the same final, made up by the course coordinator, not by the individual instructors. With sections of twenty to twenty-five students, this instruction was quite expensive. The coordinator, therefore, after experimenting with several different instructional methods, moved to a partial PSI format. Two hours a week are devoted to a mass lecture, attended by all students. The other two hours are spent in one-hour classes of about forty-two students, supervised by an instructor overseeing tutors, who are each assigned seven students. The tutors give individual attention to each student; the instructor gives quizzes, grades assignments, and acts as a liaison to the faculty giving the lectures. There has been no effort to make the course modular or self-paced, although the final exam is still given twice during the semester. The component of immediate feedback is minimized. The tutorial format, however, enables those students who pass the first-level, arithmetic course within the first four or five weeks of the semester to enter the upper-level course and perhaps finish both courses within one semester.

The reading and writing courses have been organized in the more conventional lecture-class discussion method, although with the establishment of a Reading Resource

Center, each of the reading classes now spends one hour of class time a week in the laboratory. There, students' problems are diagnosed and individual programs worked out so that the students may spend extra time in the center, if they wish, and progress as fast as they can.

Freshman Seminar, as might be expected with a group-advising orientation, is conducted mostly through small-group discussions. The two coordinators, one from each of the sponsoring offices, have been developing a decision-making game and other simulation techniques, so that the classes are by no means just "rap sessions." In addition, some sections visit the library, and many invite department chairmen, administrators, and heads of other services in to discuss various aspects of college life. A written project and final examination are also required.

After the initial work of developing the remedial courses and incorporating them into the college curriculum was completed, it might be supposed that the future would be concerned with refinement of the curriculum, evaluation of success, and continued efforts to improve instruction. This did not prove to be the case, however, because of another unforeseen occurrence.

The Hunter College Senate mandate of May 1973—that all Hunter students had to demonstrate proficiency in reading, written English, and mathematics—prompted by the change in transfer policy within CUNY (as explained in chapter 5), meant that suddenly the remedial departments had to expand their courses greatly, had to offer sections in the evening (since many of the transfer students were evening students, whereas the entering freshmen were almost exclusively day students), and had to deal with an older population. Credit for remedial courses was not awarded to transfer students, which caused the additional problem that many of them resented having to take the courses, for no credit, after having completed two years of college and perhaps even remedial courses in their previous colleges. The resulting hostility in the classroom toward the teachers became a great problem.

It may seem hard to understand how transfer students can need remediation at the level given our freshmen straight out of high school, until one considers the distance some of these students had to go. The preparation of students allocated to the community colleges, who comprise the large majority of our transfers, is almost always significantly below that of students allocated to Hunter. To bring them close to the college-entrance level is a mammoth task and is about all the community colleges can do in the time available. We now have to complete the job.

The self-paced arithmetic course had the fewest adjustment problems. It was easily expanded, and highly motivated students could exit quickly. The problem-solving course, in its new tutorial form, also made few changes, although transfer students were often resentful of having to take it if they had already finished all of the science courses necessary for the Hunter degree. The Senate therefore confirmed its mandate that the skill level exhibited by passing Problem Solving in the Sciences was necessary for all Hunter degree holders.

The Developmental English Program has attempted several innovations with respect to the transfer students, on the premise that these students are somewhat older than freshmen and have at least managed in college-level courses, although perhaps not as effectively as they might have, had their skills been better. Special sections of both the reading and writing courses have been set up for transfer students, taught more nearly than usual on a self-paced basis. In reading, for example, a program is tailored to the student's problems, and the student then proceeds at his or her own pace at the Reading Resource Center, coming to class periodically for consultation and testing. Likewise, the writing instructor initially works individually with each student on an assessment of the problems to be mastered, and then lets the student proceed individually to complete satisfactorily the required number of papers. One instructor experimented with making tape recordings of comments about papers, which the students could listen to at their convenience. This sounds like a good idea, but the instructor found that it was more time consuming than writing comments on the papers and did not seem to be any more effective from the students' standpoints in achieving an understanding of the critical analysis of the papers.

In Summary

We have found that the compensatory philosophy, although seemingly kinder and easier on the egos of the students involved, indeed is harder on them, for it forces them to flounder on their own to make up for inadequacies they often do not even know they have. It also is dishonest, in that it seems to tell students that they are able to function satisfactorily, when indeed they are not. It places them in courses for which they are not prepared and offers little or no help for their dilemma. By requiring them to make up deficiencies on their own time, it also takes no account of demands on their time outside of school, which often are considerable. And finally, it overlooks the fact that people need some sort of structure in order to function best. The college has recognized this, offering courses with syllabi and course requirements for most students and allowing only the most outstanding to register for unstructured independent study courses, yet it turned around and said that the least well prepared of its students had to accomplish the hardest tasks of all—acquiring skills not learned elsewhere—on their own.

Providing remedial help for underprepared students is, therefore, the only way to go, once the students are in the college. Whether or not college is the proper place for this remediation to take place is an entirely separate question, and one which Hunter is not in a position to decide. We had to take the students at whatever level they came to us and either give them the best help we could or else set the revolving door in motion and require them to make it on their own. CUNY's commitment was to the former.

Instruction in remedial college courses needs somehow not to duplicate what has been ineffective in the high schools. This is the hard but most challenging aspect of the situation. The atmosphere of the college, where students are treated as young adults capable of making decisions, rather than as children forced by truancy laws to be in class, can contribute to developing motivation in the students who must take remedial courses, but the courses themselves have to generate excitement and a sense of purpose. The self-pacing of our arithmetic course is one way of accomplishing this. The attempts of the English faculty to devise new approaches for transfer students are another. We need to do more.

Another alternative, which is to turn the problem back to the high schools, is, on the surface at least, the ideal solution, but probably the most difficult and the least viable. We would not have the problem if the school systems had been able to deal with it. But we cannot cast the entire blame on the school systems of the country. Experts in many fields are at a loss to explain in any simple way the causes for the almost universal deterioration of students' ability to read, write, and figure, but they seem to agree that there are many factors contributing to the problems and that both the schools and the parents must be involved in the cure.

8 Academic Advising

Until Open Admissions Hunter College had no formal office for academic advising. Prior to 1970 the curriculum had been structured so that new students had few choices to make during their first three or four semesters. Counselors in the Dean of Students' Office did a modicum of advising in connection with counseling students with regard to personal problems, but they were not there specifically to provide extensive assistance with students' academic affairs. The associate dean of instruction dispensed some academic advice, primarily with respect to students on probation or working their way back to matriculation via the evening School of General Studies, and handled administrative appeals on academic matters, such as requests for extensions of the time limits for handing in missing work from the preceding semester. Premed, prelaw, and preengineering advising was also performed in this office, by released-time faculty.

The inauguration of Open Admissions was the rationale for establishing the Office of Academic Advising, which opened for business in September 1971. The office drew together several functions that had been provided in various offices of the college, and added a few more. Among its services were the appeals, student standing, and special programs advising functions previously handled by the Dean of Instruction's Office, tutoring from the Dean of Students' Office, and the preregistration and registration advising begun for freshmen who were tested in the spring of 1971. Thus, although its genesis was Open Admissions, its focus was broadened to include the total student body with the exception of major/minor advising.

In order to maintain a close tie to the academic program, the office was staffed almost entirely with faculty who were released from a portion of their teaching duties. The associate dean who headed the office, as well as his assistant, who served as open admissions coordinator, were both considered full time in the office, although they each taught one course in their respective departments. Only the tutoring coordinator spent her total time outside the classroom, although certainly her tie to the academic program was direct. In addition, two staff members who had been involved with advising the nonmatriculated students in the evening were transferred into the office, and each of them taught one course in addition to advising evening students.

The faculty that were recruited for released-time advising service were among those who had volunteered to serve as Open Admissions advisers during the first year of the program. The original recommendation of the Committee on Open Admissions was that fifty to sixty faculty members be released half time so that each could take on about fifteen to twenty Open Admissions students, with whom they would meet periodically during the school year to discuss programs, advise on problems, and assist in making connections with college life. This plan looked good on paper but in reality did not work. City students, especially those who had jobs or commuted long distances, could not spare the time for these meetings, nor did their schedules always fit in with the faculty member's office hours. And students whose motivation for college was tenuous at best saw connections with faculty as threats rather than as supports. The faculty members, even with the best of good will, found that students did not show up for group sessions, and even when they did, faculty access to information about students and courses are spotty, and students' perceptions of their own progress in their classes was often faulty. Not least among the problems, it was difficult, if not impossible, to recruit such a large number of faculty members.

Experience during that first year demonstrated that advising had to be a systematic rather than a volunteer process. Having the advisers all assigned to one office, as was the case in the second year, was an improvement, but presented problems of its own. Although there were some ten to twelve part-time faculty available at various times, there was no single hour that all of them could be in Academic Advising at the same time, meaning that communication and information dissemination was almost impossible. In fact, we could not have a full staff meeting because of schedule conflicts. We finally had to schedule one for a Saturday in December, and even then not everyone could come. In addition, the faculty members were quite naturally more attached to their own departments than to Academic Advising, since their rewards in terms of promotion and tenure were dependent on their performance in activities in their disciplines rather than in a college service like Academic Advising. Hence, if books had to be written or conferences attended, Academic Advising was put aside. And finally, their service during the academic year was considered ended as of the beginning of exam week each semester, whereas some of Academic Advising's most important activities took place during intersessions and the summer months when the faculty advisers were not in school.

As a consequence, our tie to the academic program was good in theory, but administratively not feasible in the form recommended by the committee. Proof of this was that at the end of the first year all but three of the advisers decided to return full time to their departments. Some needed to strengthen their teaching records, since tenure decisions were coming up the next year; others had research projects that could no longer tolerate their absence; and one was elected chairperson of his department.

The office staff recruited a few replacements for the advisers from the faculty, but also looked for other ways to staff the office. One of the most satisfactory solutions was the recruitment of three graduate students who were in Hunter's Counseling and Student Development (CSD) program. This is a two-year master's program for training college counselors. Students must be full time, although many of them need part-time work. In essence, Academic Advising offered them two-year paid assistantships, and they gave us a measure of the consistency and stability we needed as a service organization. Employing these CSD advisers also meant that we could expand and contract the office as the size of the student body indicated; if the entering class increased one year, we could hire more, if it decreased, we could hire fewer. We could also require these advisers to work during intersession and other periods when our activities were at a peak.

Since all first-year students in the CSD program are required to spend five hours of service in a college as part of their course work, we were able to arrange that this service be either in Academic Advising or in the School of General Studies advising nonmatriculated students. Thus, we gained an additional fifty hours of service for which the graduate faculty provided supervision and training to supplement the supervision our limited staff could give.

Despite the flexibility advantages of this staff pattern, it was necessary at the same time to have some full-time staff members who could coordinate various administrative functions and give the office a continuity and dedication not possible with a completely part-time staff. We therefore gradually added a few full-time advisers, as the budget permitted, to oversee the major functions of the office. At the moment, our organizational pattern includes full-time staff for the following responsibilities: tutoring, testing and proficiency satisfaction, general advising and staff development, outreach and Freshman Seminar, student standing, appeals, special programs advising, and admissions advising. A different adviser coordinates each of these activities as a primary responsibility, but all share in the general activities of the office and act as a kind of "flying squad" during such periods as new-student registration, when we need every available staff member. Other academic advising offices might include different functions, but the principle should be the same: assign responsibility for each function to a different adviser, who then seeks assistance from the whole staff when his or her particular function is in the forefront of the semester's activities, and back this up with part-time graduate advisers who fill in the gaps.

Another decision, which is implicit in the descriptions of our activities so far, was that Academic Advising be a year-round function. Prior to 1971 all counseling/advising staff members were on faculty-appointment lines, which meant that they were not in the office during holidays, intersession, or the three summer months. Thus, all advising began after Labor Day and ended after final exams. Student problems, however, do not fit into such neat time blocks. Our system for advising and registering new students was also contrary to this schedule. All advisers, therefore, are now on twelve-month appointments.

Freshman Advising

While our staffing patterns were evolving over the last several years, we turned to our primary *raison d'être,* namely to advise the Open Admissions students. During that first fall semester we obtained lists of all the Open Admissions students who had registered. The university had identified two categories of Open Admissions students, those with high school grade-point averages under 70 (of whom there were very few at Hunter) and those with grade-point averages between 70 and 79.9. We divided these lists up among the faculty advisers, assigning some of each level to each adviser on a random basis; since some of the faculty were giving us six hours a week and others nine hours, the case loads varied. The advisers then wrote to their assigned students, requesting that they make appointments to come in to the office. Hindsight shows us to have been naive in assuming that the students would immediately show up at our door. On the contrary, we found that only about half of them bothered to make appointments, and only about half of those kept them; few called to break or change appointments.

As with the volunteer advising program of the previous year, we had to look for new ways to communicate with the students. Individual appointments, although perhaps ideal, made us play a passive, waiting role. When students did not show up, the advisers were idle during valuable appointment time. On the other hand, if students appeared at a peak period and could not see an adviser immediately, they rarely returned. We therefore scheduled a large group meeting just prior to registration for the following semester, at which we explained how to go about registering, discussed program-planning options, and answered questions. This was only partially successful; the turnout was about a tenth of the freshman class. We tried scheduling several small group meetings during the "free hours," hours for club meetings and other extracurricular activities when no classes are scheduled. A series of these meetings were set up in classrooms and advertised in the student newspapers and on bulletin boards. It was hoped that students would drop in for question-and-answer sessions, but these meetings, too, were only partly successful; some were well attended, others not. Attendance at any group meeting is problematic at a commuters' school, since only a portion of the student body is on campus at any given hour, and many come to classes and leave as soon as classes are over. We also had the feeling that the very students we needed to reach the most were the ones who were not coming to these meetings; those who came were the ones who realized that they needed additional information and knew how to seek it out.

We therefore decided to station advisers at the registration area so that as students came to register we would be available to give information. The advisers attempted to see the Open Admissions students in particular, although this was difficult, since there was no indication on any of their registration materials that they were Open Admissions students.

Another thing we tried that fall of 1971 was asking for midterm grades for all freshmen, to be used in assessing students' program plans for the spring. We found, however, that many of the instructors did not turn in midterm grades because the timing for submitting them did not coincide with their course plans. The midterm exam was often scheduled after the deadline, and without the test the teacher had little or no way of assessing the student. Also, most of the courses with freshmen in them also had upperclassmen, for whom midterm grades were not requested. Many teachers were not willing to rearrange their teaching plans merely to give us five or six midterm grades. Again, the idea seemed good but did not prove practical. We abandoned the practice after several semesters.

At the end of the first semester, we requested copies of the report cards of all freshmen and sorted them out according to performance levels. Those with satisfactory averages were presumed to be doing well. What we looked for were those who had earned few or no credits—for example, a series of incompletes and several of the neutral "Y" grades (indicating that the student needed an additional semester to complete the course work). We wrote to this latter category of students and told them to come in during their free hours the second week of the new semester. Advisers, each of whom had been assigned thirty or so students for conferences, were stationed in classrooms. We saw the students, went over their first-semester grades with them, discussed their second-semester programs, and then made recommendations for changes if such seemed warranted. The problem was that it was really too late in the semester to do any drastic changing, and there was no way of knowing whether or not the students actually made the suggested changes. The response was better than 50 percent, and we had personal contact with the students, but there was no opportunity for proper follow-through.

We had to search further for a way of getting advising assistance to the students. The Task Force on Open Admissions provided the impetus for our solution. As part of the remedial package, we devised the Freshman Seminar (discussed in chapter 7). In essence this is a mechanism for group advising. Half of the sections are taught by advisers from the Office of Academic Advising, and the other half by counselors from the Office of Student Services. The seminar is required for all students who are enrolled in two or more remedial courses; we would like to require it for all incoming students, but there is simply not sufficient staff for that. As it is, we teach some forty sections in the fall and about twelve in the spring, when there are fewer entering students. We often find that in the spring a number of students who had not been required to take the course in the fall sign up on the basis of friends' recommendations; we encourage this. We also find that advising relationships begun in the Freshman Seminar continue for several semesters until the students choose majors; that kind of connection is one of the major purposes of the course.

Topics covered in the seminar include requirements and services of the college; the grading system and class attendance requirements; how to add courses or withdraw from them; and where to get forms, financial aid, tutoring, and various kinds of information. Skills necessary for success in college, such as decision making, class participation, time management, and study skills, are covered, especially in terms of how college differs from high school. And finally, the seminar is an opportunity for students to share their experiences, problems, and excitements with others who are going through the same things; it is a chance to meet some fellow students, to perhaps make new friends, to begin to feel part of the scene.

Obviously, some of the problems we faced in relating to students would have been solved by making advising mandatory for all students. Such a move at Hunter, however, was not possible for a variety of reasons, not the least of which was lack of budget and adequate staff. The Freshman Seminar was certainly a good, if not perfect, substitute.

As discussed in chapter 6, the minimum proficiency requirements that initiated the Academic Alert system is another substitute that has been relatively successful. Yet again, because our staff is not large, we cannot require all students on Academic Alert to come into the office for an extended registration-planning appointment. Instead, we have to station advisers at the registration area, take our Academic Alert records there with us (these include test results as well as grades from previous semesters), and quickly scrutinize the students' proposed schedules in order to catch the gross problems. We can suggest that the students come in for appointments during the next semester, but cannot follow up on the suggestion. In addition, such monitoring means that a student is rarely seen twice by the same adviser, so no real connections are established. Continuing contact with the same adviser would be preferable, and is a goal toward which we would like to move.

Our experiment with calling students into group meetings after their first semester led us to institute what we call our Outreach program. Routinely, we now get copies of all students' report cards each semester. The coordinator of student standing, who deals with students on probation, receives the records of students whose averages are below 2.0, and our Outreach coordinator picks out those whose averages are satisfactory but mask unsatisfactory performance. Interestingly, we find that response to the Outreach letters is much better than response to general "come in to see us" letters, probably because of the threat involved when the students are told they are in trouble and should seek help before it gets worse. We pick up all kinds of other problems in these Outreach interviews, and they become a good source of referrals to other services such as tutoring, financial aid, and personal counseling, as well as an opportunity to help the students plan academic programs and become aware of college rules and regulations.

Expanding Services

As we gained more experience and were able to move from the immediate problems of establishing a new function to the second-level problems of refining procedures and assessing what else needed to be done, we found that our approach to academic advising had evolved in unanticipated ways. Our purpose became broader and more explicit: to try to deal with a large number of students in as personal a way as possible; that is, to individualize a mass situation and to include the total undergraduate matriculated student population of about 13,000 to 14,000 day and evening students. Our task was complicated by the fact that we were trying to reach out to a maximum number of students with a minimum of personnel.

Although our original focus was deemed to be the Open Admissions student, our definition of that student changed from the official one (based on high school grade-point average) used by the Board of Higher Education to the pragmatic one of any student who needs remedial help in reading, writing, or mathematics as evidenced by performance on the proficiency tests. This obviously enlarged the scope of our concerns. At the same time, we realized that we could not limit ourselves just to servicing students in remedial courses. Many other students wanted help with planning programs, resolving academic problems, choosing majors, and considering other options than the standard baccalaureate programs. And Open Admissions students would obviously complete their remedial courses, join the main stream of the college, and be faced with other kinds of advising problems as they progressed toward graduation.

Having gotten the testing and registration process in working order and having initiated advising for the entering students, we turned our attention to the other kinds of advising activities that appeared necessary. We began by establishing procedures so that we could act as the secretariat for the Student Standing Committee. This committee determined which students were to be put on probation, how long they were to continue on probation, and when they were to be dropped from matriculation. Although our Outreach activities were trying to keep students from ever going on probation, obviously the program could not be 100 percent successful. Nor is probation limited specifically to Open Admissions students. Academic Advising became the nexus for identifying students whose records should be considered by the Student Standing Committee, for informing the students of the committee's actions, and for working with probation students on realistic plans for improving their performance.

We divided some of the advising responsibilities with the personal counselors in the Office of Student Services. The

counselors saw students who were on continued probation or had been dropped, on the theory that students who
could not cope over a series of semesters might very well
have serious personal problems that were standing in their
way and that such problems were beyond the scope of an
academic adviser. On the other hand, the academic
advisers worked with the students during their first term on
probation, since their problems might well be more
academic in nature. Jointly, our two offices also worked
out an appeal system so that students who thought they
were unfairly dropped could present their cases first to a
counselor and then to the Student Standing Committee, if
appropriate.

At the same time, we strengthened our advising for special
programs. This included both preprofessional advising and
advising in the areas that are concerned with excellence,
such as four-year B.A./M.A. programs (the opportunity to
earn both degrees in four years), honors programs, study
abroad programs, nontraditional programs, grants and
awards, and graduate studies. Many of these areas had
been handled in previous years either by the staff of the
associate dean of instruction or through the information
written in the *Bulletin,* and therefore were left pretty much
up to the initiative of the individual student. We agreed
that information about these options for challenging
opportunities should be made much more widely available
to our whole student body—not only to those who were
well prepared when they entered, but also to those who
had begun in remedial courses. Open Admissions
students, like anyone else, should be given the possibility
of expanding their horizons and going on to things they
might never have dreamed of when filling out their applications to Hunter.

Finally, it became apparent that the admissions function
was so closely tied in with almost all of our activities that it
would be appropriate to move it from the registrar's office

to Academic Advising. Several reasons supported this decision. First of all, high school students considering college should know about the academic programs of the schools they are interested in, and the colleges should help them make the most informed decisions possible. Discussions of this nature are about academic questions, not about paperwork procedures and deadlines, and they should therefore be with someone who knows the academic program of the college.

All of our testing activities depend of course on close cooperation between the admissions and advising functions. This cooperation was fairly simple when it concerned only the freshmen, because we received our allocation of students on a specific date from the University Application Processing Center, but once we moved into testing all transfer students, it became critical. In the past, admissions decisions about transfer students could be made at any time up to about two weeks before the semester began, since registration for these students was only a few days before the start of classes. When testing was mandated, we needed time for testing and for registration advising to ensure that the transfer students needing remedial courses took them. And since we were working with each transfer student on program planning, we needed the evaluation of their transfer credits to make sure the students did not duplicate courses already taken elsewhere. All of these new advising procedures took time; the admissions decision-making process had to be shortened to give us this time.

In line with the current approaches to admissions, we began looking at other factors besides rigid adherence to a grade-point average. Consider, for example, the student who had been unsuccessful in a first try at college, but after several years in the business world with a chance to mature, now wished to return to college. We wanted to give that person a try, for such applicants have often turned into some of our best students. We needed to plug this kind of academic judgment into the admissions decision and then follow the student to make sure the decision was right. For all of these reasons we believed that admissions was an integral part of the academic advising process.

Problems and Attempted Solutions

Some of the problems we have faced in Academic Advising are those always faced by a service office in a large organization. We have made major efforts to maintain our credibility, and such efforts must continue throughout the life of any academic advising office. Since our beginning coincided with the adoption of the Open Admissions policy, our office is perceived by many of the faculty as responsible for all of the things flowing out of Open Admissions at Hunter, both bad and good. This has tended to color the perceptions of faculty members regarding our functions and value. A few believe that we espouse automatic promotion of all students regardless of performance. But increasingly, many seem now to realize that we are fighting to maintain standards and can indeed provide a valuable service for the faculty as a buffer against unreasonable student demands and as an ombudsman in resolving misunderstandings about rules and regulations.

The quality of our service, however, is only as good as the quality of the advice and information we dispense. We must therefore keep close ties to the faculty and the instructional program. In a college such as Hunter, where the faculty as well as the students are commuters and where the faculty does not have a strong tradition of getting involved in advising, the solution to this problem is especially difficult. We have tried several different approaches, each of which helps but does not completely resolve the problem.

We have visited each of the department chairmen to discuss course content and advising problems with them, and we have invited departmental representatives to meet with our staff for the same purpose. With approximately forty different programs and majors this is a time-consuming process and one that cannot be our only resource. We have held periodic meetings with all department chairmen and major advisers, but such large groups are unwieldy and not really very productive. We have visited some departments during their faculty meetings—again, too time consuming—and have met with the divisional deans on occasion to discuss mutual concerns—which reaches a very small number of people. We also have a Liaison Committee of representatives from the various divisions, with whom we meet regularly to discuss academic advising problems, but again, our discussions do not spread very much beyond the members of the committee and, perhaps, their departments.

We have developed an "Academic Advising Manual" which has been distributed to all major advisers, but those advisers do not have the impetus to use it regularly, as ours do; instead, it is easier for them to rely on their memory of how things "have always been," or to call our office when they have a problem. Letters to the faculty, outlining new regulations or explaining the various services in the college, become just one of the many pieces of paper that flow through a faculty member's mailbox. Often this material gets consigned to the "circular file" that holds material not immediately relevant to today's concerns; we all have too much to read.

Even in our own office communication is a problem. With a large number of part-time staff we are not able to have frequent regular meetings for the entire staff, nor can we immediately circulate a new piece of information to everyone five minutes after it is received. Our staff is spread not only throughout a forty-eight-hour week (we are open four evenings a week until seven), but also in three different offices on the main campus along with a branch office in an outlying location. This means that we have a problem just keeping our own staff members supplied with the latest decisions, dates, and interpretations; and the staff themselves have the problem that sometimes there is no one to ask. Although we emphasize the importance of not dispensing information unless we are sure about its accuracy, it is at times difficult to confess ignorance to a student—the pressure of a situation may demand an answer, even if one is not absolutely sure it is correct. We have used internal memos, staff meetings, departmental workshops, and blackboards with last-minute information, but we still have not solved this problem to our complete satisfaction.

One of our most important attempts to improve internal communication and ultimately communication with our public has been the reorganization of our reception–telephone answering service in our main office. We came to realize that these two functions were the nerve center of our office. Often, the first voluntary contact students have with Academic Advising (after preregistration and registration advising, when students frequently are not aware of what is happening) is either at the reception desk in our office or over the telephone. The nature of this experience can color a student's entire attitude toward the college, the value of our service, and the desire to come back or refer friends and classmates who may need help or information. A short-tempered, uncommunicative snap from a busy clerk will quickly turn students away, never to return; a friendly, understanding answer to a question, even if that answer is a firm no, will gain many friends and enable us to carry out our functions with increased effectiveness. We therefore carefully choose the people who staff our reception area and answer our telephones, looking for warmth, empathy with students, and ability to work under pressure, and we train them extensively. We also have enlarged the staff as budget has permitted, for the number of callers has increased yearly, and long lines or unanswered telephones are not good public relations.

Another innovation is that we regularly assign an academic adviser to an intake desk in the reception area to answer quick advising questions on the spot. Having an intake adviser not only provides instant advising, but also solves the problem of broken appointments. When students could see advisers only by appointment, we found that the appointment books might get filled, but there were many unkept appointments. Evidently, students would make appointments, which sometimes had to be scheduled for two or three weeks after the requests were made, and in the interim they would find the answers to their questions and no longer need the appointments. A few called to cancel, but many did not. Many advising questions are for information that the student needs right now, not two weeks hence. The intake adviser satisfies that need, while at the same time keeps broken appointments to a minimum. When a longer consultation is needed, it can be scheduled for the next day or so, and the likelihood that the student will keep the appointment is high.

Our experience with the importance of this intake/reception/information function led us to the realization that staff development and training is crucial to the effectiveness of our service. The variety of functions that are part of Academic Advising, together with the myriad rules and regulations and varied ramifications of each of them, make it imperative that everyone who answers questions (which is almost everyone in the office) must be knowledgeable, informed, and up-to-date about what is going on at the college and must also know where to go for answers if they are not immediately apparent. One of the worst problems in many bureaucracies, and this is especially true in a large college with many offices, is the person who has been sent from office to office on a wild goose chase. We want "the buck to stop" at Academic Advising, where the student can either get the answer or get a valid referral to the source of the answer.

Personal contacts are important ways of disseminating information, of course, but they only touch a portion of the student body. There is still the problem of getting the mass of information about college rules and regulations to all of the students. Our preregistration and registration advising are one kind of attempt. Group meetings have been relatively unsuccessful, partly because of our commuting population, but also because many students do not know they have a problem or need information until they get into trouble for its lack. They often do not have the time or inclination to attend a meeting just because it might be helpful to them at some unspecified time in the future; and in fact, they may be right, for until one needs certain kinds of information, being exposed to it will have little value. Audiovisual materials would probably be effective, but they are expensive and require personnel to develop them—and we are in long supply of neither money nor staff at the moment. Also, we do have problems with vandalism that would have to be resolved before we could leave equipment unattended.

Our peer advisers (as described in chapter 6) spread the word around to some extent, but they are far from being mass media. The Office of Student Services has been offering a course for peer counselors, which just lately began including several sessions on academic advising materials (at the request of the enrollees) and which we will be joining in teaching in the future, but again, the impact of fifteen to twenty new peer advisers/counselors per year is limited. We have also initiated a volunteer program for advising assistants, who are trained and then spend some time in our office and wear "Ask Me" badges to indicate that other students can get assistance from them. Finally, each Freshman Seminar has a student

assistant who helps in teaching the course, and these assistants naturally become knowledgeable about the college's
academic program and rules and regulations.

All of these efforts to better inform students—for their own
benefit and so that if their friends ask them questions they
can give accurate information or suggest where it might be
found—are good, but limited in their impact. They also
take many hours of our staff's time for training, which
keeps us from other things. The more ripples we can make,
however, the wider is our wake; and at least, the students
involved are gaining good training and experience and can
add to the amount of personal attention we can pay to our
large student body.

In Summary

We have been faced with the problem of dropping a new
function into an ongoing and somewhat settled bureaucracy during a period when the organization itself is having
growing pains, both physically and philosophically, as the
result of Open Admissions. This has meant that the Office
of Academic Advising has had to work in several different
directions at the same time in order to establish itself. We
first had to develop a whole new set of procedures for
advising the incoming students who might or might not
need extensive advising assistance because of their ignorance about college life and its demands. We then began to
consider and develop programs for the currently enrolled
Hunter students who never before had had the
opportunity to consult an academic advising office and
perhaps did not realize that they needed its services until
they were available.

At the same time, our activities were closely related to
those in many of the offices that had been in existence at
the college for a long time. Our office, the registrar, the

computer center, the divisional deans, the academic departments, student services, financial aid, career counseling, and on and on—we were all interrelated. We had to work out mutual lines of communication so that decisions made by one office and affecting another were relayed in sufficient time to enable rational planning of activities by all concerned. New functions require new relationships, and developing these is not easy in a large organization.

We have experimented a great deal, and in fact, no semester has resembled the other in terms of activities. We found new ways of dealing with old problems, or having solved one layer of problem went on to the next layer. Sometimes the ground rules were changed, often by forces outside the college itself. One of our most intriguing challenges has been finding innovative ways to accomplish our advising tasks so as to make our limited staff and budget go further; we have not wanted to be content with sitting back and wishing that things were better or ideal, but rather have tried to create a good advising system by searching for alternate ways to bypass the obstacles. In any event, academic advising is now recognized as an important function in the college, not only for Open Admissions students, but for all students.

9 Tutoring

Initially at Hunter each department was responsible for, and received funds for, the tutoring of students enrolled in its courses. The expectation at this time was that a faculty member or graduate student could bring the Open Admissions student up to par in a few sessions' work. It soon became apparent, however, that there were too many students requiring too much tutoring and that there were too few instructors and spaces for the task. The instructors who were available had insufficient time and were otherwise ill equipped to develop the required student skills. The paperwork alone was too much for the already overburdened department secretaries.

All of this, of course, happened before the introduction of remedial courses. We were all operating under the illusion that a good college (our college) could offer a modicum of extra services and successfully help the new, underprepared students to overcome their difficulties. This was not the case, but it took us a few years to realize fully just how much extra help these students needed.

A centralized tutoring office was established in 1971. Its only function was to offer course-specific supportive assistance. The office was assigned ten vacant classrooms and a small budget, and grew eventually into a comprehensive organization employing a director and assistant, a secretary, and approximately 100 tutors serving the needs of over 1,000 students per year. Most tutoring was limited to freshmen and sophomores and was available for only the first two levels of introductory courses offered at the college, with no tutoring at all in remedial courses.

During the first year of Open Admissions, the Hunter administration decided that only Open Admissions students should receive free tutoring. This decision became a source of difficulty since the majority of students who first requested tutoring were actually the better-prepared and self-motivated ones. They were secure enough to admit their problems and request help; further, they had educational backgrounds that enabled them to recognize that they were doing poorly. It was these students who were turned away, and they of course were angry and disappointed at being declared ineligible for assistance. Meanwhile, the Open Admissions students, not knowing what tutoring was or how it could help them, failed to sign up. These students were so alienated from and unprepared for their academic work that they had no way of knowing whether they were doing well or not. Poor work in college, unlike in high school, is not met with screams and admonitions from the teacher. Often, students would attend the lectures, listen with fascination, and then go on to fail their exams because they were unable to make the connection between college-level lectures and their textbooks, if indeed they had read the text. Students who had never learned the fundamentals of writing a research paper would submit subjective written work, completely unaware that this was inappropriate. This was a perfect formula for failing marks and further trouble.

So the tutoring office was placed in the position of having to turn away good students who needed help, while trying to recruit Open Admissions students who did not know they needed it. The department's solution was to limit individual tutoring and establish groups so that all students who requested tutoring could be accommodated. Requests for one or two individual sessions were invariably approved by the director, after which the student was usually placed in an ongoing group. More important, announcements of the availability of free tutoring were sent to department chairmen and to the instructors of introductory courses, asking them to encourage their students to sign up for help. Problems arose here, too, because some instructors felt threatened by the service, seeming to perceive applications for tutoring as a reflection of inadequate teaching ability. Some instructors ignored the tutoring service. But many who favored it were extremely cooperative, encouraging their students to take advantage of it. These teachers assumed a positive attitude, which further encouraged students; and many of them conferred with the tutors, making suggestions about subject matter—in effect making tutoring an extension of their courses. This situation permitted them to progress at a good pace in the classroom without having to backtrack repeatedly to explain basics. The weaker students were getting that kind of help in tutoring sessions. With the help of individual departments and instructors, more and more Open Admissions students began to utilize the tutoring service, as did the better-prepared students who were headed for graduate school.

The Open Admissions student is the victim of a cultural gap that manifests itself in every area of a college career. Tutoring uses a variety of approaches to close that gap: sitting with the student, supporting his efforts, and gradually teaching him some of what a college-oriented child has been absorbing since before kindergarten. This new student's environment has not been conducive to academic learning and thinking. He has been shoved and prodded through high school, and he suddenly finds that he is no longer being pushed along. The student is not so much interested in the meaning of a poem as he is interested in a grade, but study has not been uppermost in his mind, and giving up a party to stay home with a book is a value alien to his established life style. The student does not know that signing up for fourteen hours a week of course work actually means three times that number of hours in study and precludes, for example, a part-time job.

In defining the cultural gap of Open Admissions students, we cannot isolate the home environment of a particular ethnic group. This gap transcends ethnic backgrounds and has become pervasive in most of our public schools, where reading, learning, and contemplation are considered outmoded, egghead stuff. The gap between the college-oriented culture and the non-college-oriented culture has left the student unprepared for the new liberal arts education experience and for the new perception of his future with which he is confronted. The child raised in a college-oriented home is taught to point toward college, make the right choices, and pursue priorities that will ensure his entrance to and success in college. The college environment, however, is so strange to the Open Admissions student that he is usually unable to enjoy the mental challenge that is the professor's lifeline. Lack of respect in the home for the process of learning means that the student labors without fundamental support from his family. Although parents want their children to become "something" and may have high expectations of them, many are annoyed with their children's "doing nothing" (i.e., reading, studying). Neither the parent nor the child understands what goes into the achievement of a college education.

It is difficult for any of us to see in the students' terms how great a chasm lies between college admission and graduation. One well-meaning faculty member commented, "I cannot understand the students. Here we are, serving it up to them on a silver platter, and they don't want it." This teacher fails to understand that, although the student has the desire to succeed, he perceives college as a maze and has to be helped along what seem to be the simplest paths.

This is not to imply that Open Admissions students are lacking skills or intelligence; often, quite the opposite is true. Their world, however, is more media and computer related, more social/people organized than is our curriculum. These students are often very able indeed, but may be unable to translate this ability into the narrow prescription that is the term paper. Intelligent students who are not accustomed to organized study may not deal successfully with the formalized demands of tests and papers and may have difficulty adhering to college rules. The gaps between high school and college life, between college and noncollege cultures are such that, to the Open Admissions student, everyone seems to be speaking a new and incomprehensible language.

The introduction into the academic world of a new student population requires the introduction of remediation and tutoring activities. These are separate programs meeting distinctly separate needs. Remediation is provided in a structured course. Not a college-level course, its purpose is to review and develop skills that the student should ordinarily have learned in elementary and secondary school. On the other hand, tutoring does not attempt to teach basic objective skills, but rather, acts as a course guide and attempts to plug gaps in the student's way of approaching scholarly material. This presupposes that the student with basic intelligence needs to develop techniques with which to grasp the course material and that the learning methods acquired in high school are in part or wholly inappropriate to college.

Tutoring utilizes all of the study aids: drills, testing, reading notes, group work, discussions, etc. It teaches the student tricks, techniques, and shortcuts to which he has never before been exposed and which represent a unique kind of culture shock to the unprepared student.

Tutoring is hardly a new concept to the college-oriented student whose family and friends have gone to college. It is quite natural for these students to know what tutoring accomplishes and to utilize it when necessary. Hunter's tutoring office receives numerous calls from concerned parents whose children are preparing for SATs and other college boards. The kind of tutoring a college-oriented child needs is usually very well defined. Parents call to say, "My child needs tutoring in calculus," or "My child has problems with French." Arrangements are made, and more often than not the problem is quickly resolved. Children who attend private school, where classes are small, are in a sense tutored in the classroom. This situation allows for an easy give and take between students and teachers, avoids competitive pressures, and encourages the students comfortably to engage in mental exercise.

In the context of Open Admissions, tutoring addresses much more complex needs. Tutoring gives the Open Admissions student a personal guide to a particular course. It gives him someone to ask questions of and consult with, someone who will demonstrate and explain shortcuts, show him the ropes that will allow him to navigate through academia. Study is not an activity that the Open Admissions student knows or likes, and the tutor provides a role model that can help make studying more attractive and acceptable. Respect for and love of learning are unfamiliar abstractions; they cannot be objectively taught, but tutors having these sentiments can communicate them to students in subtle, unobtrusive ways.

The process of learning is continuous, inherent in living, and dependent largely upon individual resources. Most learning occurs outside the confines of academia and is something of which people are not consciously aware. Children have been learning all their lives, but this process frequently is not recognizable to them in academic institutions, where they see learning as a restricted activity of narrow scope. Tutoring can help students work their way into some of the academic and professional modes that may serve to demystify the college experience. Discussion groups, for example, permit the students to use their new knowledge, to personalize it, and to see how it applies to life.

The liberal arts curriculum leading to a degree seems meaningless to many students, and tutors help students make connections between their academic work and their professional aspirations. Some students, for example, want to go into nursing but do not see the necessity for studying chemistry. Their image of a nurse is of a figure in a white dress who sits in a hospital holding patients' hands. One student angrily protested having to take a reading course to improve deficient skills: "I want to go to medical school and be a doctor. What do I have to learn to read for?" Some want to be accountants and cannot understand why they are forced to suffer through music and art courses. Students can visualize the piece of paper that we call a bachelor's degree, and they have the expectation that this degree will lead to rewarding and lucrative employment. What goes into the achievement of that degree, however, is often a mystery. It is part of the tutor's task to help the student solve that mystery.

The tutor may often go through every step of the college learning process with the student—introducing him or her to the library, to the research paper, to the footnote, etc. Some students need drill and repetition in tutoring sessions because, not knowing how to study, they require the help of someone with enough patience simply to familiarize them with those methods. Other students need discussion. One student came to the tutoring office regularly each day to tell the director everything about the history course in which he was enrolled. The director finally had to tell him that, although talking to him was enjoyable, time would not permit the retelling of the entire course. "You won't listen, my mother has no time to listen . . ." was the student's unhappy reply. This student needed someone with whom he could *discuss history*, a function that the peer tutor can carry out with ease. Often the tutoring session is a study group, with the tutor in the background acting as guide. Students use the session to interact with other students, look things up, discuss questions pertaining to the course material, or sometimes, to learn ways of dealing with a particularly difficult instructor. In general, they begin to grasp there what is expected of them as college students.

Professors are often very far removed from the Open Admissions students' cultural backgrounds. It is not uncommon to hear of instructors who begin the first day of class with the announcement that students will have to wipe out everything they have learned before. Most of these students have been brought up to think in terms of outward appearances—clothes and fancy cars—and professors frequently condescend to them. They completely ignore the students' mores, while hoping that their own will be gratefully acknowledged and respected. Such is not the case, of course, and it is the peer tutor who offers empathy instead of condescension, addressing students in a way that will be heard without resistance. It is commonly accepted that people who are introduced to a new and alien discipline need support and comfort along the line. Tutoring does not purport to offer a psychotherapeutic cure, but rather just this intervention of supportive and comforting human "vibes."

One of the initial policy decisions of the new tutoring program was to employ peer tutors (one compelling reason for this was limited funds). Many of these undergraduate students were partially self-supporting and in need of money. Their previous part-time jobs were often a burden, and they welcomed the change, the chance to tackle responsibility, and the opportunity to help others while improving their own skills.

Tutors, no matter how successful in their own courses, seldom have a conscious understanding of the learning process. This understanding must be developed in training sessions. These sessions are not limited to the instruction of tutors in subject matter, for the Open Admissions student has difficulties that require more than rehearing the information already received in the classroom. The determining factor in overcoming learning problems or simple educational gaps is the quality of the tutor-student relationship. The need, then, is for tutors to develop a sensitivity to their students' problems and to make appropriate, nonthreatening responses. This is stressed in tutor-training sessions.

In addition, all tutors are interviewed by the director after they have completed four or five hours of tutoring. At this time they submit a study plan and outline for each student. Tutors are asked to anticipate the course material for the remainder of the semester. These materials help the tutors clarify for themselves what needs to be done and give the tutees a look at what will be expected of them in the future.

Ideally, academic life teaches a new way of being and of thinking. This restructuring of traditional attitudes is basic to Open Admissions, and it is those people closest in age to the students, at least sharing an interest in the prevailing popular culture, who are best able to introduce new attitudes and procedures. Students who tutor have already acquired a *modus operandi*—highly specialized techniques for succeeding in the academic world—but they are still flexible enough to accept the underprepared students. Acceptance by a peer tutor, both for what one is able to do and for what one is unable to do, is the first step in providing the secure environment necessary for learning. Professors, particularly those who display their own enormous grasps of their subject matters, tend to overwhelm students, creating greater insecurity and feelings of intimidation. The peer tutor, however, attends to detail and approaches the subject matter in manageable increments. There is a special understanding between student and tutor. A student may fail an exam with a score of sixty-four; the professor duly records this failure, but the tutor knows that this student has actually worked himself up from a potential zero. Both tutor and student know that success has been achieved, and the tutor is thus in a position to suggest that the student see an adviser, repeat the course, and improve his grade even more.

Tutors are students in good standing who have done well in the courses they tutor. Were it not for the tutoring program these students would have little or no contact with the Open Admissions students. The tutor has an interest in the subject, and this is particularly beneficial because positive attitudes toward subject matter cannot generally be transmitted except by (peer) demonstration. The Open Admissions student has an opportunity to associate with a person who is comfortable and familiar with academic work, who has positive attitudes toward study and learning, yet who comes from a background somewhat similar to his own. The actual work of the student/tutor team is academically centered, but the student will gain new insights and perceptions about the life-style as well as the work. Students and their parents often have distorted impressions and expectations of the college degree. It is often possible for the tutor to correct these misconceptions and, in the process, to communicate an understanding of the scholarly process itself.

Students who wish to tutor are asked to bring a letter from an instructor who knows them and their qualifications. They are interviewed by the program director before joining one of the tutor-training sessions in progress throughout the semester. These prospective tutors are given a written set of rules and regulations that summarize the training information (see exhibit 2).

Hunter's program employs three categories of tutors: senior, regular, and assistant. Distinctions between these categories, particularly between senior and regular, are not always clear, and the positions are sometimes interchangeable. Senior tutors are those who have worked in the program for a long time; they have shown interest, ingenuity, and organizational skills, and have developed as well as proven their own methods. They are generally excellent students majoring in the subjects they tutor. Senior tutors have a record of stability in their groups and have achieved consistently good results. One such tutor was able to leave the tutoring session entirely and have his group continue to function as a unit, helping each other to understand problems and find answers.

Senior tutors show a special interest in the learning process, and many have made worthwhile observations about ways of dealing with specific problems based on their own experiences with Open Admissions students. Generally they are consciously aware of the dynamics of the methods they have developed, and they tend to become involved in the nonacademic functions of the tutoring office, acting as peer advisers for students who have educational-planning problems. They frequently help with academic and registration advising and have thus

138

Exhibit 2

Rules and Regulations for Tutors

1. BE ON TIME.
   Make sure that you and your students know how to reach each other in case one or the other of you is going to be late or unable to come at all. Be considerate about letting each other know.

2. BE PREPARED.
   Know the material you are going to work with. Have your books and notes with you. Be sure you have done the necessary homework, reading of chapters, etc.

3. BE INTERESTED.
   The first meeting is important in that it allows you to acquaint yourself with the students. Try to discover something about their backgrounds, education, etc. Why are they coming for tutoring—for pleasure, High School Equivalency, college entrance, etc? What other skills or training do they possess? Attempt to discover your students' reading levels, study habits, ability to absorb material, learning blocks, likes and dislikes, etc. How well are they able to follow instructions and how well prepared are they for the particular course they are taking? Know as much as you can.

4. BE PATIENT.
   Learn to understand your students' particular difficulties and respond accordingly.

5. BE HONEST.
   a. Let the students know what you expect of them: co-operation, willingness to participate, promptness, doing homework.
   b. Be honest about your own shortcomings; it is important that you do not appear to be smarter than you are. There is nothing wrong with not knowing, only with appearing to know when you really don't. It is good for the tutee to watch the tutor figure out problems, look up words, etc.

6. INSPIRE CONFIDENCE.
   It is important to determine where your students are at so that you can begin with something they know. Begin where the tutee will experience success.
   a. The most important rule is to proceed in small steps of sequentially increasing difficulty toward the objective.
   b. Let the tutees know you believe they can do the work.
   c. Keep motivation high by letting them experience small successes. Don't say things like "you're wrong." Don't maximize mistakes—in fact, it is best not to call them mistakes. If the tutee does not know, try to work the problem through again.
   d. Let the tutee show you, teach you. Allow him to demonstrate some of what he's learned to others. (This is particularly effective in languages.)
   e. If a tutee is having difficulties visualizing symbols, use materials together with him and construct visible learning aids.

7. KEEP A RECORD.
   Observe the changes your students make. Record where you see difficulties lie, and what you and they are trying to do about it. The more you can take the difficulties apart to yourself, the better for your own understanding of student problems. A record of observations will help you to determine where the students need extra study and to differentiate between difficulties regarding memorization and those of conceptual understanding.

8. FOLLOW UP.
   Tutors will meet periodically with Ruth Jody to discuss progress as well as problems. The first meeting should be held after you have had five tutoring sessions.

developed an understanding of the system and the variety of areas in which students may require help. Senior tutors act as administrators, are given responsibility for organizing and coordinating all tutoring groups in a particular subject, and assign students to individual tutors when the need arises. They tutor groups of from ten to thirty students, often spending three or four hours at a time in review sessions or in preparation for special exams.

Regular tutors are good students with some free time between classes; they offer four to five hours per week to the tutoring program. Often these are preprofessional students or those interested in taking special state exams, and they wish to tutor in order to review basic subject matter for themselves. Regular tutors are assigned students by senior tutors, and they begin by tutoring individuals rather than groups. Eventually, as their competence grows, they tutor groups of perhaps four to six students. Regular tutors frequently make themselves available to students who come to the tutoring office requesting immediate help in passing an exam.

Assistant tutors are students in good standing who have an interest in a particular subject, but lack the full mastery of it that advanced tutors exhibit. Assistants work with senior tutors, doing paperwork, taking attendance at group sessions, and participating in group discussions and drill sessions. They review material with students who arrive early with questions pertaining to previous sessions.

Paperwork in the tutoring office is kept at a minimum to encourage spontaneity as much as possible and to avoid giving already intimidated students the impression that they are being checked up on. Because tutoring funds are university funds, some records and statistical data must be kept, though not the many forms and computerized records necessary for course enrollment. When a student appears to sign up for tutoring, he is asked to provide his name, address, telephone number, social security number, and the title of the course in which he requires assistance. (Students are sometimes fearful about this last item. Many ask if this will appear on their transcripts or otherwise be used to stigmatize them.) They are immediately given the telephone numbers of several tutors and told to call one to make arrangements for a meeting in one of the program's designated classrooms. As tutors acquire students and establish regularly scheduled groups, the Schwebel Chart (named after the tutor who developed it) is posted (see figure 1). Students can see at a glance what subjects are being tutored when, where, and by whom. Students may attend one or two of the posted sessions, depending on their needs. At the end of the term tutors are required to submit a form giving some information about their students' progress as indicated by exam grades.

The tutoring process attempts to teach students the art of acquiring information. A student once came to the tutoring office to say that she was really dumb and that she was not going to pass French because she could not remember the vocabulary. The director of the program sat down with her and began to help her study by covering the English words and asking the student to translate words from the French. The student was immediately struck by this simple, automatic (for the director) study mechanism: "Hey, what a great idea!" This student, and others like her, do not know how to study and are unaware of methods that college-oriented students simply take for granted. They frequently believe that intelligent students do not have to study. Their difficulties lead them to the conclusion that they are not intelligent, which makes them that much more willing to accept failure. Tutoring fills in the study-related gaps. The tutor acts as a detective: he looks at the student and at the particular course in which the student is to be tutored, and determines what the student does and does not know and why he is unable to grasp the material successfully.

Figure 1

	CHEM				BIO				PHYSICS					MATH					LANGUAGE				
	Course	Time	Tutor	Prof	Rea	Course	Time	Tutor Prof	Rn	Course	Time	Tutor Prof		Rn	Course	Time	Tutor Prof		Rn	Course	Time	Tutor	R
MON	42-102	8-9		Mary	410	30-100	3-4	Joan		42-150	3-4	Angie	309							15-101	8-9	Mike
	42-102	4-6		Joe	755	30-100	1-2	Richard	411	42-100	2-3	Ron	202							21-202	10-11	Rocco
	42-102	2-5		Steve	310				402	45-211	1-4	Richard	109							25-101	12-2	Mary
	42-102	3-4		Ruth	101					46-113	8-9	George	101									
	42-102	2-3		Jane	302																	
TUE	30-102	8-9		Joe	314	30-102	11-12	Lynette	202	45-150	7-8	Steve	109	42-150	8-9	Max		310	21-101	10-11	Ron
	30-100	3-4		Sandy	483	30-102	5-7	Angus	7/2	47-100	7-10	John	302	42-100	11-12	Chris		302	21-101	11-12	Joan
	45-150	1:30-2		Gabriel	403					47-100	12-1	Doug A.	415	45-211	11-12:30	Fred		202	21-101	12:30-1	Lynn
	47-100	11-12		Tania	202					45-100	2-3	Lucy	409	46-113	2-3	Sheri		203	21-101	2-3	Phyllis
										45-211	5-6	Nancy	501	42-110	3-4	Rocco		301	25-101	5-6	Mark
										46-113	7-8	Lucy	406	42-104	5-6	Nancy		403			
WED	42-100	9-11		Don	701	30-100	9-11	Una		30-100	7-8	Marshall	407	45-211	1-2	Joan		401	21-101	1-2	Patti
	42-100	7-8		Gail	601					30-100	8-10	Angela	402	46-113	3-4	Steve		302	21-101	2-3	Bea
	42-110	2-4		Bea	255				414	30-102	11-12	Tony	311						15-101	4-5	Rolla, Gail
	42-104	2-3		Sheri	406														45-211	6-7	
																			46-113	8-9	Doug
THU	30-100	5-6		Stu	402	30-100	7-8	Angela	202	47-100	9-10	Jim	411	40-300	10-11	Jim		403	21-202	7-8	Joe
	30-100	9:30-11		Cathy	446	30-100	2-3	Angela	411	47-100	12-2	Joe	755	40-302	12-2	Mary		411	25-101	8	Cathy
						30-102	1-3	Joan	411	45-100	3-4	Steve	302	40-300	3-4	Kim		755			
														40-351	5-6	Sarah		212			
FRI	40-300	1-3		Mary	314					47-100	11-12	Sandy		45-100	11-12	John		101	30-100	10-2	Steve
	40-302	2-4		Don	406									45-211	2-3:30	Bruce		622	30-100	2-3	Joel
	40-300	2-3		Sandy	403									46-113	4-5	Marian		223	30-102	4-5	Judy
	40-351	8-9		Joe	310																

The tutor's primary goal is to motivate the student to interact with the material, a task which the lecturing professor cannot be expected to accomplish. Motivation is stimulated by small achievements rather than by half-successful attempts at large ones. Helping students develop a willingness to study is one of the tutor's most difficult tasks; perhaps the most painful for the student who expects the tutor magically to make him know and understand that which he could not grasp before. Students often assume that just being present for the tutoring session will make them learn. The truth is bitter, and students are frequently hostile to the tutors, accusing them of unfriendliness or even stupidity. This accusation can, of course, be threatening to tutors, especially when they themselves are not professionally secure in their knowledge. Giving the right answers, however, is not the purpose of tutoring. In fact, tutors are encouraged to admit fallibility in order to help the students recognize that knowing all the answers is not the *sine qua non* of learning—that it is the process itself that is important and must be developed. It is particularly valuable for students to see that even their tutors must look up answers or struggle with difficult problems. Knowing that the tutors have no special or magical abilities makes students feel more confident and less intimidated.

The tutor-training sessions mentioned earlier emphasize the need for determining the precise nature of student problems. Students may have trouble with chemistry because they lack the necessary background in algebra. They may have difficulty understanding a subject because their reading skills are not adequate for a particular text. More often it is simply unfamiliarity with the nature of study. "I've read the material, but I don't understand it," is a common complaint of students who do not realize that even top-notch students may require five readings of the material before they reach an understanding of it. Prepared students know this from experience, but the

Open Admissions student, not knowing it, becomes discouraged: "There is something wrong with me, I don't understand, I am dumb, I give up. . . . Now explain it all to me."

One student came to see the director of the program asking to change her history tutor because he had failed to make her understand the material. The director offered to work personally with the student, and asked for her textbook so that they could look at it together. The student responded without any embarrassment that she did not have a book: "I don't have time to read books." Disappointed, angry, and frustrated, the student left the office complaining that she had an exam the following day and was not getting any help. Tutors are taught that in such situations it makes no sense to give the student a lecture on the importance of reading books, doing assignments, etc. Often, tutors will simply use the tutoring hour to sit quietly while the student reads one chapter several times over, by way of demonstrating that there is simply no way around the necessity of reading the book. As the tutor and student work together, the student may learn that the only way to get through college is to begin by plodding along. He finds it rewarding, finally, to know the chapter and to be able to answer questions about it.

Thus, the tutor's first responsibility is to confront students with the unpleasant fact that nobody can study for them, that the tutor is not there to do the students' work. While every effort is made in the office to maintain a comfortable and relaxed atmosphere conducive to study, the student must remember this harsh reality: no one else can do your work. The tutor offers only advice, explanation, and encouragement.

Often there is a temptation on the part of the tutors to act as psychiatrists and become involved with the students' personal problems. This is discouraged in the training sessions, in which tutors learn to assume an attitude of productive sympathy: "I know you have problems at home, that your mother has five children and is on welfare. I sympathize with you, but there is nothing I can do about that. All I can do is help you with physics, so let's get to it." Callous as this seems, it is essential that the student focus on the work at hand. There are, moreover, other counseling services available at Hunter, with counselors on hand who are qualified to deal with emotional difficulties. Students who come for tutoring in anthropology and instead give tutors their entire life history may be attempting to avoid the work. Training sessions help prepare the tutors for such behavior.

Tutor-training sessions also emphasize the importance of regularity in study habits. Open Admissions students, particularly those who work to help support their families, do not always recognize the need for hours of study outside the classroom, nor is their home atmosphere particularly conducive to such study. Studying does not bring in the much-needed three dollars per hour, and it is difficult to sustain one's study when there are no immediately visible rewards and no role models. The student who sits with a book in a chaotic household will not generally receive special consideration because he needs to study. In fact, he may feel somewhat out of place when everyone else is caught up in the "real" human struggle to survive. Professors are often cool to the students, and their grades are not sources of pride, so it is essential that the student learn from his tutor that sitting with a book *is* acceptable behavior and that study time *is* productive and ultimately rewarding.

Being on time for tutoring sessions is stressed, for it shows that the tutor has respect for his and the student's time. The commitment is, at first, technical—be on time, be prepared, get right to work—but eventually the student learns that time is valuable and that study time is useful.

This developing attitude can be communicated to the student's family, which will hopefully begin to consider and respect the student's effort.

Tutors are encouraged to prod the students to explain what it is, specifically, that they fail to understand; the next step is to sit silently while the students formulate questions. Formulating questions activates thought processes and allows for a give-and-take between student and tutor. In groups it stimulates exchanges among the students and encourages them to help themselves and each other in a supportive environment.

Tutors learn not to dwell on mistakes or even necessarily label incorrect information as mistaken. They are advised against approaching the subject matter as it is approached in the classroom. They are encouraged instead to return to the most basic aspects of the subject, to find a level which is familiar and understandable to the student, and to proceed from that point.

Tutors try to place their students at the blackboard as often as possible to let them experience some degree of role reversal. In the classroom it is the professor who uses the blackboard, and in tutoring sessions students are given the opportunity to perceive the work from this other perspective. Using the board allows students to feel confident and knowledgeable; they are teaching their tutor. This is part of the process whereby students develop the ability to speak up, ask questions, and generally expose themselves intellectually, beginning in a noncompetitive, nonjudgmental situation.

Of course, tutors learn a great deal as well. They, too, develop greater confidence; they learn how to conduct groups, how to keep records, how to confront students and faculty, and how to deal with hostility and disappointment. Tutors learn how to divide their time, devise better programs, and do research more effectively. As they recognize some of the shortcomings in their students' educations, their own shortcomings become more apparent. They begin to solve their own problems and become less inhibited about asking questions pertaining to their own work. It is very much a mutually profitable situation.

10 Maintaining Standards

One of the most often heard criticisms aimed at any Open Admissions policy is that educational standards will be diluted and that the academic degree will therefore be rendered meaningless. The validity of this argument is contingent upon how the institution involved defines and then implements Open Admissions. If the policy is perceived as a vehicle for automatic progression to graduation from the particular institution, then yes, Open Admissions will indeed denigrate the value of the education provided by that institution. If, on the other hand, the college opens its doors to all but then requires each student to "fish or cut bait" in the first semester (by passing the freshman composition course, for example), then the education certainly is not diluted, but the policy is empty; it in no way gives previously underprepared students a fair chance at proving themselves.

It seemed to us at Hunter that we had to put ourselves somewhere in between these two stances. We had to try to build up the skills that had not been learned by our students during their previous twelve years of schooling, but we could not pass students if they did not acquire those skills, nor could we subject other well-prepared students to classes taught at the lowest level of competence in order to drag the underprepared through somehow. If we did not make every effort to maintain and even improve the level and quality of the education we offered, the degree earned would not be worth the effort.

We therefore moved in several directions to ensure both that standards would be maintained and that Open Admissions students would be given opportunities that they had never had before. The first step toward the achievement of that goal was the development of remedial courses in an effort to keep the underprepared out of classes for which they were obviously not ready. This restriction has the additional advantage of not discouraging students who realize they cannot handle the course material but who do not know where to turn for help.

In another direction, the provost and the various divisional deans have worked with department chairmen and faculty to remind them continually of their role in the institution's effort to maintain its standards. Faculty are crucial factors in keeping standards high by means of their grading and attendance-keeping practices and also in their strict requiring of students to adhere to academic regulations. No advising office in the world can enforce regulations if the faculty members are not willing to refuse to accept late papers, to give "Fs" when earned, or otherwise to maintain their own academic integrity in the classroom. Certainly this is difficult; students do exert pressures on faculty members to bend or break the rules, and often the personal situations of some of our students are heartrending. There are, however, avenues for dealing with some of these problems: Academic Advising, when necessary, can be the "bad guy," and students with personal problems can be referred to trained counselors for help.

The retention policies of the college are another important ingredient in the maintenance of academic standards. Hunter was not exempted from the upsets of the late sixties and early seventies—our students closed down the school for much of the spring 1970 semester. This experience left its mark on both the faculty and students involved; for a while there seemed to be a general overreaction to the problems, a feeling that regulations were indeed too constrictive and that students should be treated as adults and therefore be allowed to determine their own standards. This produced an almost apologetic stance on the part of many among the faculty and administration with regard to their past behavior, along with a determination to be completely receptive to what were perceived as more progressive policies. When this reaction was coupled with the initiation of Open Admissions, which produced its own sort of guilt feelings, the pendulum swung too far to the pole of permissiveness.

In addition, because of the 1970 upset, all grades had to be withheld for at least a year, to give students and faculty members a chance to determine what the course requirements would be and then allow the students time to complete any agreed-upon work assignments. Thus, all decisions about probation and dropping from matriculation were suspended for a year. Without grades from the spring 1970 semester no averages could be calculated and no judgments could be made about whether incompletes were made up on time or not. The Student Standing Committee could not even meet until the summer of 1971, a year and a half after its last meeting; and even then, it would not make drastic cuts without giving the students at least a chance to make up deficiencies. Since the intersession between fall and spring semesters is always a difficult period in which to take mass actions, it was not until June 1972 that the Student Standing Committee could begin to function effectively, and by then the backlog was tremendous. For two years standards had not been applied rigorously. Word about such laxness gets around among the students and promotes even greater apathy toward following regulations. Combine this situation with the entrance of a large group of students who were unfamiliar with the nature of college regulations altogether, and you encourage, albeit not consciously, an attitude on the part of many students as well as faculty that the rules and regulations no longer mean anything.

It took time to reverse this trend and get the word out that students would be dropped and that probation is indeed a serious matter. The dedication and willingness of the faculty members on the Student Standing Committee to work long hours for several weeks after the end of each semester has put teeth into the retention requirements. The degree to which the advisers and counselors support the committee's actions also indicates commitment to standards. It is hard to say no, but we must—and we have.

The faculty, administration, and advising and counseling staffs must all cooperate in adhering to all of the college regulations about class attendance, grading, minimum and maximum credit loads, course prerequisites, and degree requirements. If not, the regulations become meaningless and might as well be erased. One of Academic Advising's functions is to identify which of these regulations are breaking down and to bring that information to the attention of the proper Senate committee, which can reconsider the merit of a regulation, or to the attention of the appropriate administrative office. This feedback function is very important. Academic advisers are often the first ones to sense when regulations are unnecessarily binding or too vague. We have, for example, worked with the registrar to make sure that regulations about credit loads are enforced. We also brought the problem of the Incomplete grade before the Academic Requirements Committee of the Senate, having found that the grade was being badly abused. Any large bureaucratic system needs an appeal mechanism for making exceptions to rules and regulations when warranted, and Academic Advising's appeal process provides this avenue; it also is a good place for spotting regulations that are honored more in the breach than followed. This kind of appeal/feedback function must exist in any institution that seriously wants to maintain standards.

Another area about which we became concerned over a year ago was that of academic progress. In our Outreach activities, as well as in the deliberations of the Student Standing Committee, we saw case after case of students who had spent several semesters at the school and yet had completed only a few credits. Some, for example, had attempted the same remedial course three or four times without success, had taken a few other courses such as physical education or perhaps foreign language courses in their native tongue (all of which they passed), but still had not really gotten into the heart of the degree program. Technically, these students were not on probation, since their grade-point average was 2.0 or better, but they were getting nowhere. We brought this problem to the Academic Requirements Committee, which in turn developed a series of minimum progress requirements that were passed by the Senate and became effective in February 1976. Students who do not complete a given number of credits each year can now be placed on probation and are subject to being dropped if they do not show improvement. Now, both level and amount of academic work are considered to be components of successful academic performance, and failure in either area is grounds for warning action. Obviously the progress requirements for students who require remediation had to be somewhat more flexible than those for students who were adequately prepared, but the requirements are there, are explicit, and must be fulfilled.

Relevant to a discussion of standards is a consideration of what it is we are trying to measure and how we go about measuring it. For example, we can say that our grade-point averages have remained high and therefore assume that standards are high, without considering the fact that perhaps students are being passed through courses without satisfactorily completing the work. Retention statistics can be subject to the same criticism. If students who are unable to handle the work are kept in college merely to swell the numbers graduating from a class, then a harmful situation is being masked. Inherent in an effort to maintain standards, therefore, is a willingness on the part of the institution to agree that college is not for everyone and that students should justifiably be counseled out as well as assisted in remaining. An important function of the advising and counseling offices in carrying out their responsibilities toward the maintenance of standards is sympathetic but firm work with the student who does not belong in college, helping that student to leave without bitterness or a sense of failure, but rather with the realization that the exposure has been valuable. This is, of course, especially true in a school with Open Admissions students, many of whom have been encouraged to attend college for all the wrong reasons. These students should feel as free to leave as to enter.

There is also much concern about the level of student work, particularly written work, evidenced in discussions pertaining to Open Admissions and academic standards. Problems such as grade inflation, lack of writing skills, restructuring (read "watering down") of courses and of the curriculum to meet student needs are often blamed on Open Admissions in schools where this policy is in effect. These are, however, problems now common to most institutions of higher education. Many of them are the result of social change and societal pressures over which education has little control but to which it must respond as a social institution. Open Admissions should not be forced to bear the burden of blame for them, nor can it be held entirely responsible for correcting them. At the same time, we should always be ready to assess these pressures and judge when they may be valuable. Rigid adherence to standards for standards' sake can be as detrimental as no standards.

In summary, commitment to high-quality education seems to be the key to the success of any educational system. It is possible, and in fact necessary, to discuss Open Admissions and the maintenance of standards in the same breath. Indeed, if we do not, the one becomes a joke and the other an empty promise.

11 Perspectives

Mention the words "open admissions," and all kinds of visions are conjured up, depending upon the background of the audience. To some the words mean the automatic lowering of all standards, not just admissions requirements. To others they mean opening the floodgates to permit certain ethnic and minority groups into previously reserved territory, whether or not they deserve entry. To a few they are the means of solving all or most of society's most pressing problems, economic, political, and social. To a different group they are merely a euphemism for another "rip-off" by the establishment, an empty promise for the true equality of opportunity that those in power have no intention of fulfilling.

One of the tasks to which the City University of New York as a whole, and each of its colleges as semiautonomous bodies, had to turn was a practical definition of what each of us meant the Open Admissions policy to stand for. As a university-wide policy, it became a measure of access to higher education, accomplished by overhauling admissions requirements throughout the system. Previous preparation, in terms of courses taken, became irrelevant,

155

as long as a high school diploma or its equivalent was earned. Beyond that the university took several innovative steps. The traditional criterion of high school grade-point average was applied, but a new dimension was added with consideration of a student's ranking in class. In this way an applicant could be compared either with all other high school graduates throughout the city on the basis of grade-point average or with fellow students in the same school on the basis of class ranking. This latter local comparison was intended to compensate for the differences in grading practices, caliber of the teaching, and student bodies among the diverse high schools in the city.

A second variation adopted by the university was in the manner of assigning students to community versus senior colleges. Because the demand for seats at the senior colleges outstripped the available vacancies, cut points for both grade-point averages and class rankings had to be established as a means of giving priority for admission to the schools most in demand. This practice had the effect of perpetuating the elite nature of the senior colleges and was therefore considered by many to be contrary to the true spirit of Open Admissions. To overcome this objection the university allocated to each senior college a group of students who wished entrance into the senior colleges but were not technically eligible for admission. In other words, every attempt was made to admit students to the colleges of their choice—senior or community—and thus give them a chance to prove that their expectations for themselves were possible even though their past performances would not have predicted it.

Finally, the university agreed to allocate the resources necessary to mount an extensive and intensive remedial effort to bring the underprepared students up to the point where they could handle college-level work. The university was under no illusion that the new student population could make it on its own and decided that the university itself must bear some of the responsibility for helping the students to "pull themselves up by their own bootstraps" in order to succeed in college. This commitment was unique in the history of education.

In this context Open Admissions is merely a new link in the chain of the educational history of the United States as it has been moving from universal primary education through compulsory secondary education to mass higher education. Like all educational movements in this country, it is tied in with larger political and social trends and is very much an outgrowth of the upheavals of the 1960s. It is the response of one societal institution to dislocations in other social institutions.

Furthermore, what the university has done in the name of Open Admissions would undoubtedly have been necessary even if there had not been such a policy. The same problems will have to be faced by others in the future, not only those in large urban areas but also those in rural areas that may thus far be largely untouched by much of what we have seen in the last five years. We are hearing from all over the country about concern over students who cannot read or write and who cannot add and subtract without the use of a pocket calculator. Even the most prestigious and selective institutions in the country are voicing these complaints and searching for ways to react to them. As higher education faces future generations of students, many of the actions Hunter and the other CUNY colleges have taken to deal with Open Admissions will be appropriate in other settings. It is to our good that Open Admissions has forced us to examine what we are doing at an early date.

It is easy to say that colleges should not be presented with these problems, that skill development is the responsibility of the high schools, or better still, of the primary grades. This is true, but we have to take the students where they are, and they are on our doorsteps. It is easy to say that someone else should do it, but hard to force them to do it. We can and have cooperated with New York City's Board of Education in pilot projects and experiments in the high schools to try to change these patterns, but we cannot wait for the results; we have to work with the students now. Changes must take place on many levels simultaneously.

The philosophy of the university's approach to Open Admissions set the tone of Hunter's response to the new set of problems presented by this change in policy, although our solutions were at the same time colored by our own particular history and traditions. Because of our high entrance standards in the preceding years, our entering students had been generally well prepared and eager to attack college on our terms. We assumed that the new students coming to us would be somewhat similar, although lacking in basic skills that they would immediately absorb. We quickly found out how wrong we were. Not only were their skills lower than we expected, but they exhibited little enthusiasm for correcting these deficiencies or for engaging in the educational process as we offered it.

As we gained experience, we were forced to change our definition of an Open Admissions student from one who came to us with a low record of past performance to one whose skill proficiency was not up to par. Although we did not see it at the time, such a definition is congruent with the basic Open Admissions philosophy that students' past performances are not as important as their current achievements and latent potentials. Our task therefore became to ensure that all students either had or attained the reading, writing, and mathematics skills that would be required in the courses they would encounter in pursuit of a degree.

This emphasis on competency fed right into our determination that the quality of Hunter's degree must be maintained. Any lowering of the standards would denigrate both the faculty and the college that awarded it and would cheat the students who received it. The whole college had to participate in these efforts. Faculty members were responsible for course content and grading standards; the Senate had to keep constant surveillance of academic rules and requirements, including criteria for retaining or dropping students who performed poorly; and administrative offices had to be vigilant in implementing the academic policies set by the college.

Statistics can be deceptive in such efforts. Low rates of attrition, for example, can mask the fact that students are being pushed through whether or not they deserve it; high attrition, on the other hand, can mean that the "revolving door" has been set in motion.

Thus, we all had to define in as objective a manner as possible how our subjective judgments about quality could be translated into viable programs and policies. Open Admissions touched the whole college in one way or another and made all of us rethink what we had been doing and where the college should be heading in the future. Many new programs and courses have resulted; increased efforts at interdisciplinary cooperation are apparent in recently approved courses; and new relations with the varied organizations in the city have been developed. Much of this would have occurred eventually, but Open Admissions speeded it up, for the changed student body made us all more aware of the changing composition of the New York City population and, we hope, more responsive to their emerging needs.

As these efforts tended to increase cooperation among various parts of the college, they seemed to break down some of the barriers erected by departmentalization and specialization and encouraged by the rapid growth of the last five years. Strong feelings of being "one big family" had existed when the faculty and staff were small, but these feelings were dissipated when the doubling of the student body necessitated the hiring of many new faculty members and the addition of a lot of new service offices. The need for all of us to consult with one another on how to confront the new problems facing us tended to offset this depersonalization to some extent and made us realize that conscious efforts to humanize our bureaucracy were necessary. Recognition of the value of turning college resources in on the college itself to solve some of its problems accelerated this process. We began to realize that there were many resources in the college—both faculty expertise and student energy—that could be channeled through course projects into meeting some of the challenges faced by the college, and that could at the same time provide the students with valuable experience in structured, sheltered learning situations comparable to those they would later experience in the "real" world.

The college response to Open Admissions, although necessarily immediate when the policy was so hastily adopted in 1970, has nonetheless been developmental. We were completely unprepared for the immensity of the problems we faced, but by taking them one at a time, we have gradually worked through several layers. There are more to come. It is not always easy to face a new set of challenges each semester, but such a situation to some extent is characteristic of the whole world around us. Learning to deal with these challenges, learning the meaning of flexibility, can therefore be of value to all of us. On the other hand, we have seen that seeking emergency solutions to last-minute decisions is not to be confused with flexibility; plans that must be put into effect in haste are wasteful and hard on both us and the students. Forces outside the college have often forced us into this position, and although we try to plan for contingencies, it has frequently been impossible to foresee their dimensions or even to foretell their occurrence. Avoidance of such situations is to be preferred.

Our experience with Open Admissions students cannot but impress us with the tremendous stick-to-itiveness of many of them. They have overwhelming odds to overcome, and the fact that they are willing to make the kinds of sacrifices they must in order to get an education demands our admiration and respect. The process of education must be a two-way street, and those that make it fully realize that necessity. That they are successful, even if the number is small, is inspiring.